Jim Curry,

Marty Bergen

MARTY SEZ

Bergen's Bevy of Bridge Secrets

By Marty Bergen

Magnus Books

Magnus Books
34 Slice Drive
Stamford, Connecticut 06907

First Printing: September, 2001

Library of Congress Catalog Card Number
2001118235

ISBN 0-9637533-8-X

Dedication

To the wonderful game of bridge.

CONTENTS

BRIDGE BOOKS BY MARTY

Better Bidding with Bergen, Volume One (1985)

Better Bidding with Bergen, Volume Two (1986)

POINTS SCHMOINTS! (1995)

More POINTS SCHMOINTS! (1999)

Negative Doubles (2000)

Introduction to Negative Doubles (2000)

For information on ordering additional copies of this or other books by Marty (or Larry Cohen's new CDs), please refer to pages 159-160.

call 1-800-386-7432
or e-mail mbergen@adelphia.net

ACKNOWLEDGMENTS

Manuscript prepared by Patty Magnus.

My very special thanks to: Caitlin, Cheryl Angel, Cheryl Bergen, Gary Blaiss, Larry Cohen, Dennis Daley, Ned Downey, Terry Gerber, Pat Harrington, Steve Jones, Mary and Richard Oshlag, Helene and Bill Pittler, David Pollard, Avrom Pozen, Jesse Riesman, Maria Rios, Susan and Rufus Rhoades, Jeff Rubens, Nancy Stamm and Ralph Wesselman.

The Official Encyclopedia of Bridge — Fifth Edition by Alan Truscott, Henry and Dorthy Francis.

THE PERFECT GIFT

If I Knew Then, What I Know Now (2001)

If you have enjoyed and benefited from Marty's "Bergenisms," you are in for a real treat. In his newest book, Marty turns his refreshing "learn, while having fun" approach away from the bridge table to the more important game of life.

With his usual wit and clarity, Marty provides a bonanza of enlightening tips based on the greatest teacher of all — experience. Here's an example:

> Never be afraid to speak up and ask for what you want. Going through life wondering, "what if," is a lot worse than having been denied and moving on.

♠ ♡ ◇ ♣

Need a head start on your holiday shopping and/or gift giving? Don't wait another moment. Turn to pages 159 -160 and order your own personalized copy. If you mention *Marty Sez*, you can deduct $2 and receive free shipping.

IN THE BEGINNING

The idea for this book came from students and readers who requested bridge tips which were short, catchy and easy to remember. Many of the tips were taken from material I have used in my teaching over the past 25 years.

Because there are so many more where these came from, I intend to write many more books using different tips with a similar style.

If you have suggestions for future tips, I welcome your participation. Feel free to:

E-mail your suggestion(s) to me at:
mbergen@mindspring.com
or
Mail your ideas to:
Marty Bergen
9 River Chase Terrace
Palm Beach Gardens, Florida 33418

If I use your idea, I will thank you with a special acknowledgment in the book. And, if you are the first to come up with that idea, I will also thank you with a free copy.

STOP – READ THIS

1. **VOB** stands for: Enough **V**alues to **O**pen the **B**idding, but not much more.

2. The player with the bidding decision to make is indicated by three question marks — ???. For consistency, South is always that player, and his hand is the one displayed.

3. According to established bridge writing, every bidding diagram must begin with West.

West	North	East	South
—	—	—	1NT
All pass			

The dashes are place holders, and in the example above, show that the auction did not begin with West, North or East. The dealer was South. The "—" does not indicate "Pass."

MARTY SEZ BIDDING STYLE

Opening Bid Style

Five-card majors in 1st and 2nd seat.
Light opening bids, based on The Rule of 20.
1NT opening bid — 15-17 HCP.
2NT opening bid — 20-21 HCP.
2♣ opening — strong, artificial and forcing.
Weak two-bids in diamonds, hearts and spades.
Preempts may be light.

Responding

Limit raises — all suits.
Jacoby transfers and Stayman after notrump.

Slam Bidding

Blackwood — traditional, not Roman Key Card.

Competitive

Michaels cuebid, Unusual notrump.

Chapter 1

GETTING OFF
ON THE RIGHT FOOT

KNOW THY PARTNER

While it is necessary to master your partnership's conventions, it is crucial to understand your partner's style.

You need to know what to expect from partner before you can make good bidding decisions. Keep in mind that it is not necessary for you and partner to have identical bidding styles. In fact, it is impossible.

In the situations below, you must know what partner is likely to do. With a close decision, does he:

- Open light? (If he relies on *The Rule of 20*, the answer is yes.)
- Preempt aggressively?
- Overcall aggressively?
- Make light takeout doubles?
- Dramatically change his style when vulnerable?

By the way: It is essential to be consistent — "to thine own self be true." Whether you are a solid citizen or loose as a goose, stay in character. Dealing with a chameleon is just too tough.

THE LAW OF THE LAND

You are always safe bidding to the level
equal to your side's number of trumps.
This is known as The Law of Total Tricks.

Although "always" is a word to be avoided in bridge,
The LAW is more accurate than any bridge player
you (or I) know, and it even transcends vulnerability.
Applications of this essential principle are endless.

West	North	East	South
1◇	1♠	2♡	???

♠ K7643 ♡ 7 ◇ 85 ♣ 98642

Bid 4♠. Adding partner's five spades to your five
gives you a 10-card fit — so jump to the four (10-trick)
level. Even if 4♠ (doubled) goes down — not to worry
— the opponents must have an easy game or slam.

West	North	East	South
—	—	Pass	1♡
2♣	2♡	3♣	???

♠ AQJ ♡ 876532 ◇ 74 ♣ A2

Bid 3♡. I have seen stronger suits, but our six trumps
plus partner's three totals nine. Sometimes, bridge is
an easy game.

A Class Act

It is hard to play like a champion, but easy to behave like one.

A CHUMP

gives "free" lessons

sides with opponents

berates partner

dwells on bad results

makes partner wish
he were elsewhere

is in his own world

thinks he knows it all

insists on playing only
his favorite conventions

A CHAMP

does not preach

sides with partner

treats partner
with respect

moves on

allows partner to enjoy
the game

knows that bridge
is a partnership game

is willing to learn

is open to partner's
suggestions

No Reason to Stall

"He who knows, goes."

If you know what the final contract should be, bid it.

West	North	East	South
—	—	—	1♠
Pass	2♣	Pass	???

♠ Q87432 ♡ Q3 ◇ — ♣ AKQJ8

Bid 4♠. You have gorgeous clubs, but so what? You want to play in 4♠, period.

West	North	East	South
Pass	2NT	Pass	3◇ (transfer)
Pass	3♡	Pass	???

♠ 6 ♡ KQJ95 ◇ J9863 ♣ 82

Bid 4♡. Because of your great hearts, you should insist on the **major-suit** game.

West	North	East	South
—	Pass	1♡	Dbl
2♡	2♠	Pass	???

♠ 53 ♡ K6 ◇ AKQJ74 ♣ A84

Bid 3NT. On a heart lead, all you need from partner to score this up is the ♠A or the ♣K. That's not too much to expect after his free 2♠ bid.

TAKE A HIKE

Taking a walk between rounds is often
the best remedy for your bridge woes.

There are times when you must get away from
partner and/or your opponents. You have probably
just gotten a bad result. Don't sit around playing the
martyr or glaring at partner. As soon as you get a
chance, just excuse yourself and leave. It does not
matter where you go — the restroom, outside, the
water fountain and "in circles" are all fine choices.

I discovered this technique the hard way early in my
professional career. I was playing with a client who
turned out to be rather obnoxious. He was obviously
not interested in learning and spent his time lecturing
me, and the opponents, on the error of our ways.

One day I just couldn't stand it any longer. As soon
as we finished the round, I was "outta there." I went
outside for some air and did not return until the next
round was called. I can't say that I looked forward to
returning to the "battle," but at least I had preserved
my sanity. And, although the money was good, I put
a quick end to our arrangement. Life is just too short.

By the way: Taking a walk to relieve a stressful
situation has helped me in many other situations.

SOME FOR ME, SOME FOR YOU

Bid aggressively when your partnership's assets are evenly divided. Proceed cautiously when they are one-sided.

1) *North*
    ♠ 752
    ♡ 1075
    ◇ A7
    ♣ J10975

3NT
Lead: ♠Q

    South
    ♠ A1063
    ♡ AQJ
    ◇ K862
    ♣ AK

2) *North*
    ♠ A75
    ♡ A107
    ◇ A7
    ♣ J10975

    South
    ♠ 10632
    ♡ QJ5
    ◇ K862
    ♣ AK

On hand 1), the 26 HCP are divided 21-5 and dummy has exactly one entry. Unless the ♣Q falls, you are limited to two club tricks. Even if East has the ♡K, you can't finesse twice. Dummy is "useless," so you are playing "**one** against two." Down you go.

On hand 2), the 26 HCP are split 13-13. What a difference! Communication between the two hands is a breeze. Now that dummy has become an active participant, the **two** of you are ready for battle. Win the ♠A, unblock the ♣AK, lead the ♡Q, and relax.

THIS DUMMY IS NO DUMMY

When dummy tables his cards, he should
hold on to the suit that was led and put it
down last.

Why should he do that? To force declarer to look over
the other three suits before playing to the first trick. It
is uncanny how many makable contracts are lost
when declarer plays too quickly at trick one. In fact,
entire books have been devoted to the subject.

Most players are so excited to become declarer that
as soon as dummy is tabled, they are off and running.
Even if they are one of the five best players in the
world, they can't play effectively at that speed.

By the way: There are lots of little things you can do
to help partner when tabling dummy. Alternate colors
— do not put the spades next to the clubs. Place the
higher-ranked cards closest to you. Make sure to
space the cards neatly so that partner can easily see
how many you have in each suit. You get the picture.

THRIFTY IS NIFTY

When in doubt, make the "cheapest" bid.

Trust me, this works. Here is a good example.

West	North	East	South
Pass	1◇	Pass	1♡
Pass	2♠	Pass	???

♠ J3   ♡ A98542   ◇ Q9   ♣ AJ10

Partner's jump shift was game-forcing, but you have loftier goals. Over 2♠, most players would routinely rebid their six-card heart suit. However, 3♡ is "expensive" (it bypasses 2NT, 3♣ and 3◇) and misdirected (your hearts are probably too weak for 6♡ if partner has a doubleton).

You should make the cheapest bid, 2NT, which has many advantages. It assures partner that clubs are under control, and allows him to:

- Rebid 3◇ with a six-card suit. That would be wonderful news — 6◇ here we come.

- Bid 3♡ with three-card support. Your six-card suit is now looking good, as is a heart slam.

Cheap bids — they lead to good auctions, better contracts and best of all, very happy partners.

Chapter 2

HAND
EVALUATION

100 Honors — Awesome

Any suit containing four honors can be bid as though it were one card longer.

West	North	East	South
—	—	1♣	???

♠ AKQJ ♡ 75 ◇ K742 ♣ 943

Overcall 1♠. As a matter of fact, I am so impressed with these spades that I would open 1♠ in any seat.

West	North	East	South
—	—	—	1♡
Pass	1NT	Pass	???

♠ AQ43 ♡ KQJ108 ◇ 843 ♣ 2

Rebid 2♡, even if playing 1NT forcing. You should be delighted to bid this lovely heart suit again.

West	North	East	South
—	—	1♠	Dbl
Pass	2◇	Pass	???

♠ 63 ♡ AKJ10 ◇ AQ4 ♣ KJ53

Bid 2♡, promising at least 17 HCP. Yes, you have only four hearts, but they are so exquisite that you are treating this as a five-card suit.

THE FORGOTTEN HONOR

The 10 is an honor card. Make sure you treat it with respect.

In fact, when your 10 is accompanied by a higher honor, it becomes especially significant.

If you have two "accompanied tens" in suits that are at least three cards long, you should add one point to the value of your hand. In fact, two tens can be more valuable than one jack — they strengthen two suits.

Choose your opening bid with each hand below:

♠ AJ108 ♡ 85 ◇ AQ109 ♣ 752
Open 1◇. Take a look at those two spiffy suits. This is not merely a "balanced 11-count."

♠ 43 ♡ AJ10754 ◇ A1065 ♣ 8
Open 1♡, not 2♡. You could easily miss a game if you preempt with this nice hand.

♠ A73 ♡ KQ104 ◇ 74 ♣ KQ107
Open 1NT — proudly. With two useful tens, it is both legal and logical to call this a 15-count.

By the way: Once you add one point for the pair of tens, the first two examples satisfy The Rule of 20.

Just What the Doctor Ordered

If all you need from partner to make a game is a minimum hand with the right card(s) — bid 'em up.

The best time to apply this principle is when partner has preempted. He has limited his HCP and given you a good picture of his hand — you need little else.

West	North	East	South
—	3◇	Pass	???

♠ A6 ♡ A75 ◇ K42 ♣ 97543

Bid 3NT. As long as partner has seven diamonds headed by the ace, you are looking good.

West	North	East	South
Pass	2♡	Pass	???

♠ A64 ♡ K84 ◇ AK1086 ♣ 72

Bid 4♡. All partner needs is a good heart suit and three clubs (so you can get a ruff). If not, your tenth trick may come from diamonds. A more delicate approach (2NT) is a waste of time.

By the way: Some players make the mistake of hoping that partner has perfect cards **and** a maximum. That is not good bridge, it is greed.

I'VE GOT PLENTY OF NOTHING

When you have a fit, the value of dummy's void is equal to his number of trumps.

Many players believe that dummy's void is a juicy, five-point asset. Sorry, "it ain't necessarily so."

You pick up:

♠ 1062   ♡ —   ◇ K9642   ♣ K8752

Partner opens 1♠. You have support, two kings and a void — not bad. You may already be picturing partner ruffing all of his heart losers in your hand. Not so fast. Partner will need plenty of fast entries to his hand, and alert defenders will lead trumps once they see your void. Of course, if partner has four losing hearts, your three trumps can't possibly suffice.

Your void is worth 3 points only — one for each trump. Once we add those to your 6 HCP, your total is 9 — not enough for a limit raise. After all, "10 ever, nine never." If your ♣5 were magically transformed into the ♠5, then you could make a limit raise. With your actual hand, a gentle raise to 2♠ is enough.

By the way: Declarer's void is always worth three points. Trumping with dummy's "short" trumps is more desirable than trumping with declarer's "long" trumps.

YOU CAN'T BE TOO SHAPELY

Five-five, come alive.

Any hand with 5-5 distribution has great potential. This is especially true with good suits, and really gets exciting once you find a fit. Here is your hand for the three auctions below:

♠ K10986　♡ A10872　◇ 65　♣ 2

West	North	East	South
Pass	1NT	Pass	2♡ (transfer)
Pass	2♠	Pass	???

Bid 3♡. Because partner would not open 1NT with two major-suit doubletons, you must have a fit. That is all you need to force to game with this shapely hand.

West	North	East	South
Pass	1◇	Pass	1♠
Pass	2♠	Pass	???

Bid 4♠. Now that you have a fit, this hand is golden.

West	North	East	South
—	—	1♣	???

Overcall 2♣ (a Michaels cuebid), even if vulnerable. "5-5 come alive" also applies in competitive auctions.

A hand rich in aces should be upgraded,
even if those aces are unsupported.

In fact, if you are lucky enough to have all four, you
should count them as 17 HCP. This hand certainly
looks good to me.

♠ A976   ♡ A5   ◇ A842   ♣ A64

However, I can't tell you how many times I have heard
players show their disdain for a hand like this by using
the phrase "aces and spaces." Personally, I'll take an
ace, as opposed to a pair of queens, any day.

Despite their identical distribution and point count, the
next two hands are worlds apart.

♠ A72   ♡ A83   ◇ A964   ♣ 654
Open 1◇. Always open a hand that has three aces.
This is a logical adjustment to The Rule of 20. Partner
will be delighted with your three quick tricks.

♠ QJ7   ♡ QJ8   ◇ QJ62   ♣ QJ5
Pass. You should not even dream of opening a hand
that has no quick tricks. Queens and jacks just do not
hold their own.

KNOW YOUR LIMIT

An ideal limit raise in a major includes four trumps and 10-12 distribution points.

Whenever you raise a suit, it is wrong to count HCP alone — players who say "7-9" or "9-11" are really confused. So, when deciding if your hand is strong enough for a limit raise, just add your short-suit points to your HCP. With four trumps, add one point for a doubleton, three for a singleton and four for a void.

	West	North	East	South
	Pass	1♡	Pass	???

♠ 652 ♡ 10964 ◇ 2 ♣ AK732
Bid 3♡ (3◇ if playing Bergen Raises). You have ten distribution points, a strong five-card suit and good heart intermediates.

♠ QJ ♡ 7432 ◇ Q954 ♣ KJ8
Bid just 2♡ (3♣ if playing Bergen Raises). You have no aces and an ugly spade holding.

♠ 754 ♡ J8654 ◇ AQ72 ♣ 6
Bid 4♡. With a weak hand that includes five trumps and a singleton, always raise directly to game.

By the way: If you choose to make a limit raise with only three trumps, you are not doing anything wrong.

Honors in partner's short suit(s) are usually not worth much.

Even an ace becomes a questionable card when partner is void. Although the ace is not "wasted" opposite a singleton, it is not "working." Honors in partner's long suits are working because they build tricks. Honors in partner's short suits are on vacation.

How do you know when partner has a short suit? He shows one when he:

- Doubles for takeout.

- Makes a splinter bid.

- Bids a suit after your Jacoby 2NT response.

- Overcalls the Unusual notrump or Michaels (showing **two** short suits).

Sometimes the logic of the auction — by friend or foe — will pinpoint partner's shortness.

West	North	East	South
1♡	Dbl	Pass	???

♠ A9765 ♡ KJ4 ◇ 872 ♣ 93
Bid only 1♠. If your heart honors were located in another suit, you would jump to 2♠.

Chapter 3

OPENER'S DECISIONS

BID MORE WITH LESS

When you open 1♡ or 1♠ and partner makes a limit raise, never pass if you have a singleton or void.

This is true, no matter how light you open.

West	North	East	South
—	—	—	1♡
Pass	3♡	Pass	???

With each of these hands, opener should rebid 4♡.

♠ 8　♡ K10854　♢ AJ98　♣ K54

♠ 98　♡ Q97532　♢ 6　♣ AKJ4

♠ AK75　♡ 98542　♢ KJ53　♣ —

Compare this hand with those above:

♠ K7　♡ KQJ94　♢ Q74　♣ Q53
Pass. Don't be seduced by your trumps. Your aceless hand and 5-3-3-2 distribution are huge turn-offs.

By the way: Of course, when opener has "extra values," he will be delighted to bid game even without a singleton or void.

A MINOR DILEMMA

With four diamonds and five clubs, open
1♦ only when your minimum opening bid
includes strong diamonds.

You will usually open 1♣, following the important
principle that it is best to open in your longest suit
whenever possible.

♠ K6 ♡ K5 ♦ A963 ♣ QJ942
Open 1♣. You will have an easy 1NT rebid after
partner responds 1♡ or 1♠.

♠ Q ♡ KJ10 ♦ K742 ♣ A8542
Open 1♣. After the expected 1♠ response, you
will bid 1NT. If partner responds 1♡, you are happy
to raise to 2♡.

♠ 86 ♡ A6 ♦ AQJ8 ♣ Q9743
Open 1♦ — look at those lovely diamonds. If partner
responds 1♡ or 1♠, you will bid 2♣.

By the way: If you open 1♣ and partner responds
1♡, 1♠ or 1NT, your 2♦ bid is a reverse. It promises
at least 17 HCP, and more clubs than diamonds.

6—4—6

When opener has 6-4 distribution, he
should usually show his four-card suit
before rebidding the six-bagger.

You can remember this by chanting "6-4-6."

West	North	East	South
—	—	—	1♠
Pass	1NT	Pass	???

♠ AQ7643 ♡ 6 ◇ KQ53 ♣ A8
Bid 2◇. Unless partner passes, you should rebid
spades at your next turn.

♠ A98654 ♡ K1082 ◇ — ♣ KQ2
Bid 2♡. This is not a one-suited hand. After you
opened 1♠, partner's 1NT response can include
a lot of hearts.

♠ KQJ1085 ♡ A642 ◇ 7 ♣ J7
Bid 2♠. These spades are so good that you must
make an exception in this case. You want to play this
hand in spades, period. Ignore your other major.

FLAT AS A PANCAKE

Once you open 1♣ with a totally flat hand (4-3-3-3), NEVER introduce a four-card major at your second turn.

Obviously, if partner responds in your four-card major, you will raise. Otherwise, just rebid 1NT with 12-14 HCP, or 2NT with 18-19.

It does not matter if your major is strong, or whether you have stoppers in all the unbid suits. With a very flat hand, you should always be thinking notrump.

West	North	East	South
—	—	—	1♣
Pass	1♢	Pass	???

♠ QJ87 ♡ K74 ♢ 1083 ♣ AK3
Rebid 1NT, not 1♠.

♠ A94 ♡ KJ72 ♢ AJ10 ♣ KQ9
Rebid 2NT, not 1♡.

♠ AKJ10 ♡ Q94 ♢ Q73 ♣ J92
Nice spades — not relevant. 1NT, of course.

DON'T WAIT FOR A FOURTH

Opener can raise a 1♡ or 1♠ response to the two level with just three trumps.

It is better to make a three-card raise than to:
- Rebid a five-card suit;
- Bid notrump with a singleton in an unbid suit;
- Reverse with a minimum opening bid.

West	North	East	South
—	—	Pass	1♣
Pass	1♠	Pass	???

Bid 2♠ with each of these hands:

♣ AQJ ♡ J33 ◇ 73 ♣ AJ834
I refuse to rebid 1NT or 2♣.

♠ KQ6 ♡ AQ87 ◇ 9 ♣ QJ753
Once again, you have no alternative.

♠ 432 ♡ AKQ8 ◇ 7 ♣ A6543
Yes, your spades are pathetic However, you simply are not strong enough bid 2♡.

OUT OF BALANCE

When you open 1♣ or 1◇ and partner responds 1♠, it is often right to rebid 1NT with a singleton spade.

West	North	East	South
—	—	Pass	1♣
Pass	1♠	Pass	???

Rebid 1NT with each hand below:

♠ 2 ♡ A952 ◇ 8643 ♣ AKQ3
It was correct to open 1♣ with these lovely clubs and horrific diamonds. But your fate is now sealed — 1NT is your only possible rebid.

♠ 9 ♡ AQ82 ◇ KJ2 ♣ A8463
Don't rebid 2♣ on a five-card suit. A bid of 2♡ would be a reverse.

♠ A ♡ AKJ3 ◇ 652 ♣ 96532
Our forefathers opened 1♡ so they could bid 2♣ after a 1♠ response. That was very sensible, but it is not the modern style.

It's not Necessarily Over

When partner responds in a new suit, opener's jump to game is NOT a signoff.

Once opener shows a terrific hand, responder is welcome to bid if he has extra values.

West	North	East	South
—	1♣	Pass	1♠
Pass	4♠	Pass	???

♠ K97643 ♡ 5 ◇ A73 ♣ Q95

Bid 4NT. Don't even consider passing. After partner has promised four spades and 20 distribution points, even 7♠ might be laydown.

West	North	East	South
Pass	1♡	Pass	1♠
Pass	4♡	Pass	???

♠ KQJ74 ♡ K3 ◇ A9542 ♣ 2

Bid 4NT. Partner committed us to game despite our possible six-count. He must have a great suit and a hand that is just short of a 2♣ opener. We have a great dummy for him.

PLAY IT AGAIN, SAM

In a competitive auction, opener can rebid a four-card minor once it has been raised.

In general, rebidding an unsupported five-card suit is not recommended. However, once partner shows support, everything changes. Now, even a four-card suit may suffice.

West	North	East	South
—	—	—	1◇
Pass	2◇	2♠	???

♠ 6   ♡ A975   ◇ AKJ4   ♣ 9872

♠ 73   ♡ A3   ◇ KQ108   ♣ A8532

♠ 94   ♡ KQJ9   ◇ J1054   ♣ AK6

Because partner's 2◇ bid denied a four-card major, you are sure that the opponents have at least eight spades. Therefore, you should compete by bidding 3◇ with each of the hands above.

Chapter 4

RESPONDER'S DECISIONS

A MINOR FIB

If you are stuck for a bid, it is okay to lie about your length in a minor suit.

West	North	East	South
Pass	1♣	Pass	???

♠ 532 ♡ 762 ◇ AQ9 ♣ 8743

Because you have six points, you must keep the auction open for partner. Now what? 1NT feels wrong without any major-suit stoppers. Raise to 2♣? Not with this square hand and lousy clubs. Therefore, you should respond 1◇, the lesser of evils.

West	North	East	South
1♠	Dbl	Pass	???

♠ Q7542 ♡ 985 ◇ 92 ♣ 1084

This is not fun. You certainly can't pass with such lousy spades. 1NT would promise at least five points — you don't have that.

If you are considering 2♡ — forget it — that is a very dangerous lie. Takeout doubles are all about finding a **major-suit** fit, and if you bid hearts, you run the risk of encouraging partner. That is the last thing you had in mind. Therefore, respond 2♣. Partner can't possibly get excited about your **minor suit**.

DANCE WITH WHO BRUNG YA

With a choice between raising partner's 1♡ opening bid to 2♡ or responding 1♠ — "support with support."

In order to appreciate the danger of suppressing your support, let's begin with a hand that has no fit.

♠ K7542   ♡ 65   ◇ 43   ♣ KJ108

West	North	East	South
—	1♡	Pass	1♠
Pass	2◇	Pass	???

Despite your less-than-magnificent "support," you must take a preference to 2♡. Your spades are ratty, you are an ace short of 2NT, and 3♣ is forcing.

Because the delayed 2♡ bid shows only a doubleton heart, it is crucial to make the immediate raise when you really do have support.

♠ KQ986   ♡ Q87   ◇ Q6   ♣ 975

♠ AQ1082   ♡ 1043   ◇ Q83   ♣ 54

Both of these hands contain nice-looking spades, but that is not relevant. You have the values and support for a single raise, so bid 2♡ right now. Tell your story in one bid — that is what good bidding is all about.

JUST ANOTHER FOUR - CARD MINOR

A 2♣ or 2♦ response to 1♡ or 1♠ can be
made with a four-card suit.

West	North	East	South
Pass	1♠	Pass	???

♠ 9 ♡ KQ63 ♦ A754 ♣ KQ92				Bid 2♣
♠ Q9 ♡ AQ6 ♦ A843 ♣ AJ86				Bid 2♣
♠ K6 ♡ A1075 ♦ KQJ3 ♣ 842				Bid 2♦

Also worth knowing:

- The above is true whether or not you are
  playing 1NT forcing and/or 2/1 game forcing.

- Because responder may have bid a four-card
  suit, opener should raise with three-card
  support only when his "trumps" are very strong.

- A 2♡ response to 1♠ shows a five-card suit.

By the way: Responder needs more than a four-card
minor in competitive auctions and as a passed hand.

DO WE HAVE A FUTURE?

Answering "Yes, no or maybe" to "Do we have a game?" will often help responder decide what to do.

West	North	East	South
Pass	1◇	Pass	1♡
Pass	1♠	Pass	???

♠ Q9 ♡ KJ86 ◇ A74 ♣ QJ43
You have an opening bid opposite an opening bid, so **YES** you belong in game. Jump to 3NT.

♠ 976 ♡ AQ109 ◇ 8 ♣ 86543
Once opener fails to jump to 3♡ or into a new suit, you have **NO** game. You should pass.

♠ J1076 ♡ AK762 ◇ 9 ♣ J54
It sure was nice of partner to bid spades. You are happy to jump to 3♠, saying partner, "**MAYBE** we have a game."

NOT READY FOR A COMMITMENT

When responder's major is raised to the
two level, he should not jump to game with
only four trumps.

Responder must remember that opener may have
raised with three-card support.

West	North	East	South
Pass	1♢	Pass	1♠
Pass	2♠	Pass	???

With invitational values (or better), responder should
bid a new suit or notrump rather than insist on game
in a possible seven-card fit.

♠ A765 ♡ AQ ♢ J98 ♣ Q653
Bid 3NT. If opener has four spades, he will bid 4♠.

♠ Q843 ♡ 83 ♢ AK2 ♣ AQ72
Bid 3♣. Although you may end up in 4♠, you should
not commit your side to spades yet. A forcing bid of
3♣ will allow your side to explore other contracts. If
opener then bids 3NT, you will be delighted to pass.

I'M GAME FOR ANYTHING

After your partnership has bid three suits, responder's bid of the fourth suit is an artificial game force.

This is referred to as fourth-suit game forcing, and does not apply by a passed hand.

Responder uses this important convention when he has an opening bid, but needs information from opener to determine the best game (or slam). This (alertable) bid says nothing about his holding in the fourth suit.

West	North	East	South
Pass	1♦	Pass	1♠
Pass	2♣	Pass	???

With each of the following hands, you should bid 2♡, quite uncertain about the best contract.

♠ AQ97 ♡ 832 ♢ A54 ♣ AQ9

♠ KJ942 ♡ A4 ♢ 75 ♣ KQ82

♠ AQ8542 ♡ K74 ♢ 8 ♣ AJ5

HAVE YOUR CAKE AND EAT IT, TOO

When your partnership has bid three suits at the one level, responder's jump is NOT forcing — it is invitational.

This is one of the nicest byproducts of playing *fourth-suit game forcing.* When responder has VOB (**V**alues for an **O**pening **B**id) or better, he forces to game by bidding the fourth suit. With a slightly weaker hand (11-ish points), he is content to invite game by jumping at his second turn.

West	North	East	South
Pass	1♣	Pass	1♡
Pass	1♠	Pass	???

♠ A63 ♡ K743 ◇ A104 ♣ 964			Bid 2NT
♠ 75 ♡ AQ73 ◇ 92 ♣ KJ932			Bid 3♣
♠ 98 ♡ KJ942 ◇ AQJ43 ♣ 2			Bid 3◇
♠ 87 ♡ KQJ943 ◇ A75 ♣ 63			Bid 3♡
♠ KQ74 ♡ 98643 ◇ A5 ♣ 54			Bid 3♠

When partner promises a six-card suit, you can support him with a singleton honor.

West	North	East	South
—	1♡	Pass	1NT
Pass	3♡	Pass	???

♠ 964 ♡ Q ◇ 9543 ♣ AK852

Bid 4♡. You are delighted with your heart honor and not tempted to bid notrump with your weak spades and diamonds.

West	North	East	South
—	1◇	Pass	1♡
1♠	2◇	2♠	???

♠ 832 ♡ AQ543 ◇ K ♣ 8754

Bid 3◇. You are unwilling to defend 2♠, and 3◇ must be a playable contract.

West	North	East	South
—	2♠	Pass	???

♠ A ♡ A5 ◇ AKJ9 ♣ 875432

Bid 4♠. You definitely have enough for game, and your ♠A will be more than adequate support.

Chapter 5

NOTRUMP
BIDDING

THE GOOD, THE BAD AND THE UGLY

Not all balanced hands with 15-17 HCP qualify for a 1NT opening bid.

1NT is a very descriptive opening bid. You tell your story (distribution and HCP) and avoid awkward rebid problems — all in one breath.

However, that does not mean that every time you pick up a balanced hand with 15-17 HCP, you should just blindly open 1NT. Instead, you must take a close look at your HCP, as well as the entire hand. Upgrade or downgrade accordingly and then choose your opening bid.

♠ QJ62 ♡ QJ2 ◇ QJ7 ♣ KQJ
Yuck — open 1♣, not 1NT. These 15 HCP are nothing more than a pile of junk. Queens and jacks are very overrated. Compare this with:

♠ K1098 ♡ K74 ◇ K87 ♣ AQ7
Open 1NT, happily. You have the same shape and HCP as the hand above, but you have great spade texture and three quick tricks (as opposed to one).

♠ A103 ♡ K3 ◇ AQJ104 ♣ K63
Open 1◇. This hand should be upgraded to at least an 18-count because of the gorgeous diamonds.

When bidding notrump, give yourself extra
point(s) for a long suit.

The following are logical additions:

Five-card suit	one point
Six-card suit	two points
Seven-card suit	four points

West	*North*	*East*	*South*
Pass	1NT	Pass	???

♠ 962 ♡ K53 ◊ 72 ♣ AQ954
Bid 3NT. Nine HCP plus one length-point totals 10.
That is enough to raise a 15-17 1NT to game.

♠ A96 ♡ QJ5 ◊ Q7 ♣ 96432
Bid only 2NT. No extra point for these pitiful clubs.
Common sense dictates that we be ready to adjust
our "formula" for suits like this one.

♠ 53 ♡ A6 ◊ A82 ♣ AQJ983
Bid 6NT. You have 15 HCP. Add two for the six-card
suit. Now, make the positive adjustment of adding an
extra point for your superb clubs. The final total is 18
— enough to make the logical jump to slam.

No Major Interest

Don't bid Stayman with 4-3-3-3 distribution.

Even if opener has a fit for your four-card major, you don't rate to take more tricks in a suit contract than in notrump. Therefore, responder should ignore his major and raise to the appropriate level of notrump.

West	North	East	South
—	1NT	Pass	???

♠ 652 ♡ K762 ◇ J98 ♣ KQ6
Invite with 2NT.

♠ Q743 ♡ Q76 ◇ K65 ♣ AJ3
Raise to 3NT.

♠ AK74 ♡ QJ3 ◇ A74 ♣ Q102
Invite slam with 4NT.

♠ AJ2 ♡ Q983 ◇ AQ5 ♣ AJ10
Jump to 6NT.

JUMP!

When you open 1NT and partner transfers, you should usually jump with four trumps.

When you accept the transfer, you are not showing support. You are just following orders, and may have a doubleton in responder's suit. When opener does have four-card support, he should do something dramatic, and jumping opposite partner's possible Yarborough certainly qualifies. You don't need 17 HCP for this jump, just a hand that "looks good" for playing in responder's suit.

West	West	East	East
♠ KQ106	1NT	2♡	♠ J8743
♡ A86	3♠	4♠	♡ 73
◇ 62	Pass		◇ A8753
♣ AQ92			♣ 5

West may have only 15 HCP, but with spades as trump, this is no minimum. East had not considered game, but once opener showed great support, he correctly reevaluated his 5-5 distribution and ◇A.

The reward for a well-bid hand was a nice game bonus when West played carefully. Once he realized there was no reason to draw trumps, making 4♠ was a walk in the park.

When partner transfers and you have four trumps, do not jump with an "ugly" 17-count.

West	West	East	East
♠ K652	1NT	2♡	♠ J8743
♡ KQJ4	2♠	Pass	♡ 73
◇ Q2			◇ A8753
♣ KQJ			♣ 5

Despite his 17 HCP and four-card support, West should not jump to 3♠. He should downgrade his hand because it has:

- No aces.

- A dubious diamond holding.

- Only 2 ½ quick tricks — sub-par for 1NT.

On a very good day, East-West will have only four losers, but 3♠ does rate to go down. Another problem with jumping is that when West bids 3♠, East will compound the error by raising to four.

YOU GOTTA HAVE CLUBS

A 1NT response to a 1◇ opening bid
promises clubs.

Once responder bypasses hearts and spades, and
fails to support diamonds, his 13 cards invariably
include at least four clubs. In fact, when he is not
strong enough to respond 2♣, he can even have
a very long club suit.

These hands all qualify for a 1NT response.

♠ Q93　♡ 872　◇ K86　♣ KJ98

♠ 752　♡ QJ5　◇ 63　♣ AJ1087

♠ 84　♡ A5　◇ 1042　♣ Q96532

♠ K8　♡ K7　◇ 84　♣ J876532

By the way: The one time you should respond 1NT
to 1◇ with three clubs is: when you have a balanced
hand with very weak diamonds and stoppers in the
other suits. For example,

♠ QJ6　♡ K108　◇ 8652　♣ K84

SIX EVER, FIVE NEVER

After you respond 1NT, do not introduce a suit that is only five cards long.

If responder does not have a six-card suit of his own, he should choose one of partner's.

West	North	East	South
—	1♠	Pass	1NT
Pass	2◇	Pass	???

♠ 7 ♡ K642 ◇ 972 ♣ KJ983
Pass. Taking eight tricks will be hard enough. Do not try for nine by bidding 3♣. Inviting game with 2NT is totally out of the question.

♠ A ♡ J97643 ◇ Q8 ♣ 7542
Bid 2♡ — the obvious action.

♠ J4 ♡ Q9854 ◇ J3 ♣ K632
Bid 2♠— take a preference to your guaranteed seven-card fit.

By the way: All of the above is true whether or not you are playing "1NT forcing."

HE'S GOT YA COVERED

When partner opens 1NT and RHO shows a suit, you should proceed as if opener has that suit stopped.

Trust me, he almost always will. As these examples demonstrate, responder will have insurmountable problems if he does not take this advice.

West	North	East	South
Pass	1NT	2♠	???

♠ 54 ♡ K75 ◇ A92 ♣ J8742
Bid 2NT. You don't want to sell out to 2♠.

♠ 82 ♡ 953 ◇ AQ85 ♣ AJ43
Bid 3NT. Remember, you are counting on partner.

West	North	East	South
Pass	1NT	3♡	???

♠ A3 ♡ 98 ◇ KQJ3 ♣ 97532
Bid 3NT, just as you would if East had passed.

By the way: For those adventurous souls who elect to play lebensohl, it can be helpful after a two-level overcall, but does not apply after RHO jumps.

IF YOU GOT IT, FLAUNT IT

Once partner passes your opening bid and the auction becomes competitive, you need 18-19 HCP to bid 1NT.

Partner could not even respond to your opening — he might easily be broke. You need a very strong hand to even consider trying to take seven tricks in notrump "on your own." Even 18-19 HCP might not be enough.

South should bid 1NT on each of these auctions, but I would not blame him for wondering where his seven tricks are coming from.

♠ KQ8 ♡ QJ9 ◇ AJ7 ♣ AQ87

West	North	East	South
—	—	—	1♣
1♠	Pass	Pass	???

West	North	East	South
—	—	—	1♣
Pass	Pass	1♡	???

West	North	East	South
—	—	—	1♣
Dbl	Pass	1◇	???

DEFINITELY NOT WEAK

2NT is *never* a shutout bid.

If you are considering a bid of 2NT, but desperately want partner to pass, think again.

Responder's 2NT bid:

- Is occasionally forcing;
- Usually invitational;
- But **never weak**.

West	North	East	South
Pass	1♡	Pass	1♠
Pass	2♢	Pass	???

♠ A1075 ♡ 6 ♢ 542 ♣ Q9873
Pass. You are going nowhere.

♠ Q7632 ♡ 84 ♢ 92 ♣ AJ64
Bid 2♡. With this weak hand, all you can do is take a preference — 2NT would show 10-12 HCP.

♠ KQ94 ♡ Q6 ♢ K84 ♣ J1095
Finally, a textbook example of an invitational 2NT bid.

Chapter 6

ALL ABOUT SLAM

THE MEEK SHALL INHERIT...

There is nothing wrong with the weaker hand taking over and bidding Blackwood.

Too many people believe that Blackwood must be initiated by the "strong hand." Not necessarily. The player who should bid 4NT is the one who knows that the partnership has the values for slam.

West	North	East	South
—	2♣	Pass	2♠
3♥	3♠	Pass	???

♠ KJ98653 ♡ 8 ◇ K854 ♣ 6

Bid 4NT. After partner opened 2♣ and supported spades, "the sky's the limit."

West	North	East	South
—	1◇	Pass	1♡
Pass	4♡	Pass	???

♠ K84 ♡ Q10963 ◇ K72 ♣ A9

Bid 4NT. With controls in all the side suits and a good hand, this is a classic. Opposite partner's four-card support and 20-ish points, you are happy to take over.

GREED IS A TERRIBLE THING

Once you have found a fit, strive to play slam in a suit, rather than in 6NT (even at duplicate scoring).

West	North	East	South
—	1♡	2♠	3♢
3♠	4♢	Pass	4NT
Pass	5♡	Pass	???

♠ AK4 ♡ 7 ♢ KQ85432 ♣ K7

Bid 6♢. Bidding 6NT for a higher score in duplicate would not be crazy. However, in 6♢, you will be able to ruff a spade in partner's hand. That is a trick you will not have in a notrump contract. Bid and score up your diamond slam, and let the hogs get a top if they can bid AND make 6NT.

For what it is worth, this hand was taken from a recent duplicate game. Partner had opened light with:

♠ 3 ♡ Q8642 ♢ AJ7 ♣ A632

On a 12 top, 6♢ making six earned a score of 10½. Most of the Norths passed originally, and their side played in 3NT or 5♢. By the way, 6NT down one would have scored a whopping half a matchpoint.

WHAT'S YOUR HURRY?

4NT should NOT be your first bid when partner has opened one of a suit.

Opener's answer to Blackwood will tell you NOTHING about his hand other than the number of aces (or keycards) he was dealt. Responder can always obtain that information later. If he is dealt a huge hand and his partner opens, he should make an economical bid and listen to what his partner has to say.

West	North	East	South
Pass	1♡	Pass	???

♠ AKJ   ♡ K93   ◊ KQ65   ♣ Q84

Did 2◊   not 4NT. Why?

- If partner opened light, you may not have a slam at all. You will find this out by going slowly, not by jumping to 4NT.

- If partner has two aces, you still don't know what to do — you may be off two club tricks.

- Partner's answer will not tell you whether you belong in hearts, notrump or even diamonds.

When partner opens 2♣, and you have a good club suit and a decent hand, respond 3♣ immediately.

When responder has diamonds, hearts or spades, he sometimes bids 2◊ (waiting), and then shows his suit at the three level. Fine, but you can't do that with clubs because the delayed 3♣ bid is always artificial.

- If opener rebids 2♡ or 2♠, then 3♣ by responder is an (alertable) second negative, showing 0-3 HCP.

- If opener rebids 2NT, then 3♣ is Stayman.

If responder does not bid 3♣ at his first turn, his next chance to introduce clubs will be at the four level. (Marty's note: on many of these auctions, 4♣ would be artificial.)

When partner opens 2♣, respond 3♣ with:

♠ 54   ♡ K8   ◊ 432   ♣ AJ9653

♠ 5   ♡ J53   ◊ 9864   ♣ AKJ108

♠ 76   ♡ 94   ◊ 83   ♣ AQ76542

HELP ME, PARTNER

When you know you belong in slam, but do not know where to play, jump to 5NT to ask partner for help.

This is referred to as "5NT pick a slam." In response, partner will suggest a final contract by bidding a suit with undisclosed length or strength. You will then either accept his suggestion or move on.

West	West	East	East
♠ AQJ9	1♣	1♡	♠ K105
♡ 7	2♠	3♡	♡ AJ86432
◇ AKJ	3NT	5NT	◇ Q7
♣ AJ753	6♠	Pass	♣ K

Because West has jump shifted, East knows that his 13 HCP will make slam a good bet. He rebids 3♡, hoping partner will support. West can't comply, and bids 3NT. Undaunted, East forces with 5NT and is delighted to play in spades when West shows a very strong suit.

West had no trouble making 6♠ on a crossruff. He would not have made 6♡ or 6NT.

Avoid Blackwood unless you have controls in all of the unbid suits.

This will prevent you from getting to a slam with two fast losers.

A control is "a holding that prevents the opponents from winning the first two tricks in a suit." When playing in a suit contract, aces and voids both qualify as first-round controls. Kings and singletons are second-round controls.

When you are missing any of the necessary controls, proceed by cuebidding — "cheapest" control first. You will usually establish a trump suit before beginning a cuebidding sequence.

West	North	East	South
Pass	1♢	Pass	1♡
Pass	3♡	Pass	???

♠ A6 ♡ AKJ95 ♢ K43 ♣ 762

Cuebid 3♠. Unless partner has clubs controlled, you want no part of slam.

♠ 64 ♡ AKJ95 ♢ K43 ♣ A76

Cuebid 4♣. Once you fail to bid 3♠, partner will know that although you have slam interest, you do not have a spade control.

THE GREAT DEBATE

Don't just close your eyes and bid
Blackwood — give cuebidding a try.

Let's set the scene. On one side, we have the
reigning champion — **B**lackwood 4NT. On the
other, the challenger — the **C**uebid.

Degree of difficulty: What could be easier than
4NT? (Advantage **B**lackwood)

Democracy or not: 4NT — the ultimate dictatorship.
Cue-bidders — equal rights. Both partners are
actively involved in the process. (Advantage **C**uebid)

Level: 4NT forces you to the five level. Cuebidding
can be done at the four (or even the three) level, and
allows you to stop in game. (Advantage **C**uebid)

Flexibility: You can Blackwood after cuebidding, not
vice versa. (Advantage **C**uebid — the challenger is
looking good.)

What you uncover: 4NT — number of aces (and/or
keycards). Cuebid — location, location, location.
(Game, set and match to the **C**uebid.)

By the way: Easley Blackwood preferred to cuebid.

Not Tonight, Dear

Once an opponent opens the bidding at the one level, you do not have a slam.

West	North	East	South
—	—	1♡	Dbl
4♡	4♠	Pass	???

♠ KQJ4 ♡ AJ2 ◇ QJ103 ♣ AK

Yes, you have 21 HCP. Despite that, you should pass! There are exactly 19 HCP left for the other three players, and East did open the bidding.

Partner's 4♠ bid was based on spade length and heart shortness, not HCP. There is no way he has both a diamond honor **and** the ace of spades.

For those who must know, partner's hand was:

♠ A10976 ♡ — ◇ 642 ♣ J9752

By the way: After an opponent opens at the one level, good slams are as rare as finding a needle in a haystack. However, when RHO opens in third seat, and you have the "goods," you must consider the possibility that he opened "on air."

Chapter 7

PASSED-HAND
BIDDING

Vive la Différence

Pay attention — the effect of partner's bid may change when he is a passed hand.

"I was playing with Marty for the first time — just a bit nervous, but in my lucky South seat. Wouldn't mind a Yarborough for starters. No such luck. I picked up:

♠ A ♡ A83 ◇ A97432 ♣ 652

West	North	East	South
—	Pass	Pass	1◇
Pass	1♠	Pass	2◇
Pass	2♡	Pass	???

"Now what? Well, I certainly can't pass 2♡, that's forcing (Marty's note: not by a passed hand). Can't bid 2NT with these clubs. 3◇ on that ratty suit — no way. I need four hearts to raise, but nothing is better. Aha! If I raise hearts, I will get to be dummy. 3♡ it is."

Marty bid 4♡ and everyone passed. A club was led and Patty nervously tabled her hand. "Sorry, I only have three hearts, but I didn't know what else to bid."

Marty said, "That's okay, Patty'" But LHO was not as discreet. "You should have passed 2♡ — Marty was a passed hand."

"'Passed hand? Oh no! Wow — what a difference.'"

READY, WILLING AND ABLE

In third seat, feel free to open a strong four-card major.

This strategy is most effective when you have less than 14 HCP, and a suit headed by three honors. By opening in your best suit:

- You help partner find the best lead; and,

- You make it more difficult for LHO to bid than if you had opened in a minor.

You are probably going to pass any natural bid from partner. If he raises with only three-card support, do not panic, your strong suit will see you through.

West	North	East	South
—	Pass	Pass	???

♠ AKQ2 ♡ 85 ◇ K964 ♣ J73
Open 1♠. If LHO wants to bid hearts, force him do so at the two level.

♠ AQJ5 ♡ 8 ◇ AK8 ♣ A7654
Open 1♣. Nice hand — bid your longest suit first.

By the way: Opening a strong four-card major in fourth seat can also be effective.

PUTTING ON THE BRAKES

When you have opened in 3rd or 4th seat and know that game is very unlikely, pass ASAP.

Unless, of course, you really can't stand the contract.

Remember, you have NO obligation to bid on when you have opened in third or fourth seat. If you bid again, you are not promising a good hand, but you are giving partner a second chance. If you are afraid to hear from partner, don't give him the opportunity.

West	North	East	South
—	Pass	Pass	1♣
Pass	1♠	Pass	???

♠ 974 ♡ KJ42 ◇ 5 ♣ AKJ65
Pass. If partner had responded 1♡, a heart game would still have been possible, and you would have been happy to raise. Once he responds in spades, leave well enough alone.

♠ AK ♡ 864 ◇ 532 ♣ A10542
Pass. You are going nowhere. You may be in a 4-2 "fit," but you are only at the one level.

A jump shift by a passed hand promises support for partner's suit.

This (alertable) bid shows a good passed hand with at least nine cards in the two suits. It is most often used after a minor-suit opening, is not forcing, and works well in competitive auctions.

Some players use the jump to show 10-11 HCP with no fit — they are proudly announcing that they almost opened the bidding. Big deal. All they have done is crowd the auction. It is definitely better to define the passed-hand jump shift as promising a fit. If you do not have a fit, do not jump.

West	North	East	South
—	—	—	Pass
Pass	1♣	Pass	???

♠ 8 ♡ 73 ◇ AKJ84 ♣ J8542	Bid 2◇
♠ 96 ♡ KJ654 ◇ 72 ♣ AQ96	Bid 2♡
♠ AJ942 ♡ 8 ◇ 83 ♣ K9542	Bid 2♠

By the way: After responder's jump, opener's retreat to his first suit is a signoff. His bid of a new suit is forcing for one round.

TAKE THE LOW ROAD

If you are a passed hand, and partner opens and then rebids 1NT, forget all about 3NT.

Here's the scoop. You were not strong enough to open. Partner opened in third seat, denied support for your suit and limited his hand to a maximum of 14 HCP. Where are you going?

West	North	East	South
—	—	—	Pass
Pass	1♢	Pass	1♡
Pass	1NT	Pass	???

♠ QJ6 ♡ KQ72 ♢ 643 ♣ KJ3

Pass. You passed originally because your hand was aceless and flat. The fact that partner opened in third seat did not change your cards. Take your plus score.

For your information, although partner's bidding was impeccable, he had the following 11-count:

♠ K102 ♡ 43 ♢ AKJ8 ♣ 7642

By the way: After the 1NT rebid, a major-suit game is highly unlikely. The one time it is possible is when the passed hand has a shapely maximum with both majors: ♠ A7653 ♡ AJ982 ♢ 64 ♣ 8.

When partner is a passed hand, forget about slam unless you have a 2♣ opening.

Because partner has failed to open or preempt, his strength and distribution are severely limited.

West	North	East	South
—	Pass	Pass	1◇
Pass	1♠	Pass	3♣
Pass	3♠	Pass	???

♠ 95 ♡ A ◇ AQ8542 ♣ AKQJ

Although partner promises six spades, bid only 4♠. Even if your side has no outside losers, partner would need a great spade suit to make slam worthwhile. With a suit like that, he would have opened 2♠.

West	North	East	South
Pass	Pass	Pass	2NT
Pass	3◇	Pass	3♡ (3◇ = transfer)
Pass	4◇	Pass	???

♠ AKQ ♡ J76 ◇ QJ7 ♣ AKJ4

Bid 4♡. Even if partner has five diamonds as well as five hearts, slam is impossible. He would need four of the five missing high honors in his two suits — that would add up to an opening bid.

Chapter 8

PREEMPTS —
WE DO IT

3 OUT OF 5 AIN'T BAD

You don't need 2 of the top 3 honors to open a weak two — 3 out of 5 is just fine.

1)   *North*
        ♡ 2

     South
       ♡ KQ6543

2)   *North*
        ♡ 2

     South
       ♡ QJ10987

It would not shock me to take only three tricks with the first combination. However, four tricks are guaranteed with the second.

As dealer, at any vulnerability, open 2♡ with the next two hands, neither of which contains "2 of the top 3."

♠ 43   ♡ KJ10932   ◇ 82   ♣ KJ7

♠ 2   ♡ AJ10864   ◇ J975   ♣ 84

BID ONE MORE

At favorable vulnerability, try to preempt "one more" than normal.

Too many players fail to appreciate the exquisite desirability of favorable vulnerability. When the scoring system minimizes your defeats while maximizing your victories, GO FOR IT.

You are dealer on the following hands. Your opponents are vulnerable and you are not. Yeah!

♠ J108754 ♡ 9 ◇ A54 ♣ 862

Open 2♠, your jack-high suit notwithstanding. This weak two-bid follows the principle of bidding more than others would because you are bidding when they would have passed.

♠ 4 ♡ 97 ◇ KQ9863 ♣ 9874

Open 3◇. Most players would open 2◇, but at these colors you want to "up the ante." You are also delighted to preempt at the higher level because you are short in both majors.

♠ 84 ♡ QJ109762 ◇ — ♣ J1086

Open 4♡. Although you have only a seven-card suit, your 7-4 shape and great spot cards suggest that you bid "one more."

SEVEN BAD IS GOOD ENOUGH

If the vulnerability is wrong for a preempt at the three level, open a weak two-bid.

Your preempt will still give partner useful information while disrupting your opponents. There is no law that says you can only open a weak two-bid with a six-card suit. Besides, you will not hold many seven-card suits — make the most of them.

On the following hands, you are vulnerable. Although these suits are too weak for a "normal" weak two-bid, the seventh trump compensates.

♠ Q5 ♡ K5 ◇ Q875432 ♣ K3	Open 2◇
♠ Q72 ♡ J1086543 ◇ K2 ♣ K	Open 2♡
♠ A976532 ♡ 62 ◇ K8 ♣ J6	Open 2♠

By the way: Weak jump overcalls can also be made on seven-card suits. If my RHO had opened 1♣, I would jump to two of my suit with all of the above hands, despite being vulnerable.

A MAJOR ON THE SIDE

Preempting with an outside four-card major is neither illegal nor stupid.

This is especially true when the major is weak, and the long suit is strong.

As dealer, regardless of vulnerability:

♠ A	♡ J532	◇ QJ10865	♣ 74		Open 2◇
♠ 7543	♡ KQ10943	◇ 5	♣ K3		Open 2♡
♠ 9	♡ 9864	◇ 9	♣ KQJ9754		Open 3♣
♠ AJ109743	♡ 8532	◇ 7	♣ 5		Open 3♠

However, if your four-card major is very strong, you should not preempt in first or second seat.

♠ K1097	♡ KQ7543	◇ 86	♣ 5		Pass

EIGHT IS ENOUGH

In first and second seat, a 4♡ or 4♠ preempt promises a weak hand with an eight-card suit.

If you think of a four-level preempt as a "three-bid" with an eighth trump, you are on the right track.

Unfortunately, many players open 4♡ and 4♠ with a long major suit and an opening bid. This "close your eyes and bid game" approach often silences the enemy and may even result in a "normal" contract.

However, it has two major flaws. On many of these hands, you don't belong at the four level. On others, you will preempt partner out of a good slam.

♠ KQJ76542 ♡ 8 ◇ 9 ♣ Q108
Open 4♠ with this perfect preempt, regardless of seat or vulnerability.

♠ AKJ9842 ♡ — ◇ K5 ♣ J1082
Open 1♠ in first or second seat. However, if partner is a passed hand, you should forget about slam. Now, you are delighted to open 4♠.

Sock It To 'Em

Preempt in third seat as often as possible, especially when you are not vulnerable.

- When the first two players have passed, and you have a weak hand, LHO must have the goods. A preempt will complicate his life.

- Partner could not open and you have preempted. Partner knows that your side is going nowhere, so relax, he will not bury you.

- A bid will help partner lead, a pass will not.

The auction has begun with two passes. It is your turn to bid and you are not vulnerable.

♠ 54　♡ KQJ98　◇ 9765　♣ 76
Open 2♡. A third-seat weak two-bid on a five-card suit? Absolutely — try it, you'll like it.

♠ QJ10976　♡ —　◇ 10986　♣ 854
Open 3♠ — what fun! Take that, LHO!

♠ 9　♡ J6　◇ AQ98754　♣ KJ5
Open 3◇.Opposite a passed hand, game is a long shot. This looks like a good place to play, so get there as fast as you can.

LAST BUT NOT LEAST

A fourth-seat preempt shows 9-12 HCP.

It may well be a hand you would have opened at the one level as dealer.

If you are in fourth seat with a very weak hand, you should pass the hand out and ask, "Who forgot to open?" Therefore, the only time you should "preempt" in fourth seat is when you expect to make your bid. Keep in mind that you are counting on partner to have his fair share of the missing HCP.

West	North	East	South
Pass	*Pass*	*Pass*	*???*

♠ AJ ♡ 872 ◇ QJ10976 ♣ K8   Open 2◇

♠ AQ9862 ♡ 3 ◇ 874 ♣ K103   Open 2♠

♠ Q ♡ 95 ◇ KQ2 ♣ KQ87532   Open 3♣

♠ 6 ♡ AQJ9743 ◇ K2 ♣ 432   Open 3♡

When partner preempts, you don't have to
bid just because you were dealt 13 HCP.

Once partner has preempted, you know that he has
less than an opening bid. Therefore, you need more
than an opening bid to produce a game. Of course,
the better your support, the better your chances.

West	North	East	South
—	2♠	Pass	???

♠ 95 ♡ AJ7 ◇ QJ832 ♣ KQ7
Pass. You are disappointed that partner did not
have an opening bid, but you have no game.

♠ 7 ♡ KQ8 ◇ KQJ ♣ KJ7542
Pass. Despite your stoppers and long suit, you
will not make 3NT opposite a weak hand.

♠ 10862 ♡ A98742 ◇ 4 ♣ A6
Finally, you have something to say. Bid 4♠, like a
shot. Though definitely not an opening bid, you have
shape to die for. Not many losers here, either.

FEATURE, SCHMEATURE

A 2NT response to a weak two-bid asks opener if he has a minimum. The "feature" issue is secondary.

In response to 2NT, opener rebids his suit whenever he has a minimum. He only shows a feature (an ace or king in a side suit) with more than a minimum.

West	North	East	South
—	—	—	2♠
Pass	2NT	Pass	???

♠ QJ10652 ♡ K4 ◇ 854 ♣ 63
Rebid 3♠. This hand is a minimum.

♠ AQ10943 ♡ 2 ◇ K83 ♣ 732
Bid 3◇. This is about as good as it gets. You are delighted to show your diamond feature.

♠ AQJ1097 ♡ 74 ◇ 6 ♣ J1092
Rebid 4♠. You have no feature to show, but it would be criminal to describe this hand as a "minimum."

PARTNER'S SUIT OR ELSE

When partner opens 3♡ or 3♠, forget about 3NT — either pass or raise.

Whether or not you have a fit, you should be playing in partner's suit. His weak hand will be virtually worthless in any other contract, especially notrump.

Partner's 3♡ or 3♠ preempt said: "either play in my suit or you are on your own."

	West	North	East	South
	—	3♡	Pass	???

♠ KQJ5 ♡ 7 ◇ KQJ2 ♣ K964
Pass. You can't make 3NT on your own, and in 4♡, you expect to lose at least three aces and a trump.

♠ AK73 ♡ — ◇ A8762 ♣ AK74
Bid 4♡. I have seen better "support." However, your five quick tricks should combine nicely with partner's expected five trump winners.

By the way: You would respond 3NT (to partner's 3♡) with a hand such as:

♠ A5 ♡ — ◇ K93 ♣ AKQJ8752

P.S. Don't hold your breath waiting for this hand.

Chapter 9

PREEMPTS — THEY DO IT

FIRST COME, FIRST SERVED

You can't preempt a preempt.

After an opponent opens with a preempt, a jump
overcall promises strength, not weakness.

West	North	East	South
—	—	2♡	???

♠ AKJ865 ♡ 85 ◇ AJ ♣ KJ4
Bid 3♠, inviting game. You are too strong for 2♠.

♠ AQJ9854 ♡ K5 ◇ AQJ ♣ 5
Bid 4♠. With this very strong hand, you are ready to
insist on game. Although partner will often pass, you
will be delighted if he "goes slamming."

♠ KJ109543 ♡ 3 ◇ 965 ♣ 82
Pass. Sad but true. *Any* bid would promise values.

By the way: A jump overcall in the balancing seat
also promises strength (but could be a touch lighter).

Looking Good in Your New Suit

When partner overcalls an enemy's opening preempt, your bid of a new suit is forcing.

Partner invariably has at least VOB to overcall at the two or three level. If you also have a reasonable hand, prospects for game (or slam) are bright. You would like to explore without fear of being dropped.

West	North	East	South
2♢	2♠	Pass	???

♠ Q7 ♡ AQ43 ♢ 82 ♣ AK842
Bid 3♣. You have no idea where (or how high) you are going — all the more reason to make an economical, forcing bid.

♠ J103 ♡ 82 ♢ 76 ♣ AQ9754
Bid 3♠. Your spade support is the key to this hand. Ignore your clubs.

♠ 85 ♡ Q3 ♢ AJ5 ♣ KJ8754
Bid 2NT. You have invitational values and a diamond stopper. Game is possible — let partner decide.

♠ 8 ♡ KQ10973 ♢ J742 ♣ 93
Pass, unhappily. A forcing bid of 3♡ would start something that your hand is too weak to finish.

PICK A MAJOR, ANY MAJOR

When an opponent opens 3♣ or 3♢, a cuebid shows a good hand with at least 5-5 in the majors.

Because you are forcing partner to bid at the four level, use this bid (also called Michaels) judiciously.

West	North	East	South
—	—	3♣	???

♠ AK1043 ♡ AKJ62 ♢ J8 ♣ 3
Bid 4♣ — a typical hand for this strong bid.

♠ AJ1097 ♡ AJ1098 ♢ 854 ♣ —
Bid 4♣, again. Although 10 HCP is not the norm, the great intermediates and club void make this action a standout.

♠ Q7643 ♡ J8532 ♢ A ♣ KQ
Pass. You have more HCP than in the previous example, but your major suits are puny. Hands with too many honors in their short suits are overrated.

♠ KQ1084 ♡ A98743 ♢ 9 ♣ 8
Bid 4♣. 6-5 hands don't grow on trees.

THE CHEAPEST GAME IN TOWN

When an opponent opens 3♡ or 3♠, try to avoid overcalling 4♣ or 4◇.

We would all rather play 3NT than 5♣ or 5◇, and an opponent's annoying preempt does not change that fact. However, you can't bid 3NT without a stopper in the opponent's suit — no matter how many HCP you have. But if you overcall 4♣ or 4◇, you bypass 3NT, and if partner has a stopper, you just missed the boat.

The solution is to double, even with a very imperfect hand. We call this a "Thrump" double (it is alertable). You are begging partner to bid **THR**ee notr**UMP** if he has a stopper in the opponent's suit.

West	North	East	South
—	—	3♡	???

♠ A2　♡ 853　◇ AKQJ83　♣ K5

Although 4◇ seems obvious, you need a lot of help to make an 11-trick game.

It is a lot more flexible to double. If partner bids 3NT, you will cheer (and buy him a drink after the game). If he responds 3♠ or 4♣, you will bid 4◇, and be no worse off than if you had made that bid originally. If partner jumps to 4♠, you will correct to 5◇.

A MAJOR CHANGE

When in doubt, bid **4♠** over **4♡**.

By doing so, you change the trump suit from "theirs" to "yours," without increasing the level of the auction. You deprive the opponents of a potential game bonus, while possibly securing one for yourself.

There is almost no limit to the number of applications of this principle, which is so important that it even transcends vulnerability.

With the following hand, overcall 4♠ on each auction, regardless of the vulnerability.

♠ KQJ975   ♡ 7   ◇ 63   ♣ KQ98

West	North	East	South
—	—	4♡	???

West	North	East	South
3◇	Pass	3NT	???

West	North	East	South
—	—	1♡	1♠
2♡	2♠	4♡	???

IT'S NOT UNUSUAL...

After an opponent opens with a preempt, 2NT and 3NT are natural overcalls. They are not the Unusual notrump.

A 2NT overcall shows the values for an opening 1NT bid, and promises at least one stopper in the opponent's suit. Balanced distribution is the norm.

Jumping to 3NT promises a terrific hand, and may be based on a long running minor. Partner may bid on, but only with an obvious action.

	West	North	East	South
	—	—	2♠	???

♠ AQ6	♡ K43	◇ J8732	♣ AQ	Bid 2NT
♠ K3	♡ A	◇ AKQ8654	♣ Q95	Bid 3NT
♠ 9	♡ 84	◇ KQJ98	♣ KQJ75	Bid 3◇

By the way: If you are a passed hand, you obviously can't have a natural notrump overcall. Therefore, 2NT and 3NT become "unusual," and promise the two lower unbid suits.

It Is Unusual

After an opponent opens 4♡, a 4NT overcall shows at least 5-5 in the minors and a promising hand.

This 4NT bid is a variation of the Unusual notrump. You are asking partner to bid his longer minor.

How do you decide whether to force partner to bid at the five level? Some decisions are difficult, but these factors suggest offense, not defense:

- Vulnerability and HCP.

- Your holding in the opponent's suit (a void is worth its weight in gold).

- Extra length or good spot cards in the minors.

West	North	East	South
—	—	4♡	???

♠ 8 ♡ 63 ◇ AQJ32 ♣ KQ854
Overcall 4NT, only if not vulnerable. You would be a lot happier with a singleton heart.

♠ 52 ♡ — ◇ KQJ108 ♣ KJ10983
Overcall 4NT, even vulnerable. You have a heart void, 6-5 distribution and exquisite spot cards.

A NEWFANGLED DOUBLE

A double of an opening 4♡ or 4♠ preempt is neither "takeout" nor "penalty."

It is a "card-showing double," so named because it promises "cards" (lots of HCP). It usually shows shortness in the opponent's suit, but might not include four cards in the other major.

If you believe that a double of 4♡ is takeout, saying "partner, please bid," and that a double of 4♠ is penalty, saying "partner, please pass," take a look at the following hands. RHO opens 4♡ or 4♠.

> ♠ A4 ♡ A72 ◇ KQ72 ♣ AQ93
>
> ♠ J2 ♡ AQ ◇ KJ643 ♣ AK64

You should double — no other action has any merit.

Once you make a card-showing double, partner will:

- Bid a six-card (or longer) suit if he has one.

- Bid 4♠ (over 4♡ doubled) with spades.

- Bid 4NT (takeout) with length in the minors.

- Pass and hope to go plus.

Darn those preempts, anyway.

Chapter 10

COMPETITIVE AUCTIONS

SHORTER IS BETTER

The shorter you are in the opponent's suit, the harder you should try to take action.

If RHO opens (any level) and you are thinking about stepping in, let your holding in his suit guide you.

- With a singleton or void, almost anything goes.
- With a doubleton, make your decision based on the vulnerability.
- With three or four cards, be cautious.

West	North	East	South
—	—	1♠	???

♠ — ♡ K1086 ◊ 9752 ♣ AQ975
Double — in your sleep. In fact, if East had opened 2♠, I would still double — even vulnerable.

♠ 6432 ♡ Q6 ◊ KJ52 ♣ AKQ
Don't double — only two hearts.
Don't bid 1NT — no spade stopper.
Don't overcall — no suit to bid.
Pass — that's all she wrote.

Au Naturel

When your RHO opens 1♣ or 1♢, a jump overcall in his suit is not a cuebid. It is natural and preemptive.

This is a weak jump overcall, just as it would have been if RHO had opened in another suit.

West	North	East	South
—	—	1♣	???

If you are not vulnerable, you should definitely bid 3♣ with each of the following hands. I would also make the bid vulnerable, though you may choose not to.

♠ — ♡ 864 ♢ J854 ♣ AKJ1098

♠ 6 ♡ 865 ♢ 72 ♣ KQJ9764

♠ 875 ♡ 8 ♢ A3 ♣ KJ109543

♠ Q6 ♡ 432 ♢ — ♣ AJ876542

By the way: Although 3♣ is a natural overcall when RHO opens 1♣, a 2♣ overcall would still be a (Michaels) cuebid, promising both majors.

I'M A BIDDER

With a choice between a double or a major-suit overcall, go with the overcall. (This applies at the one level only.)

If you bid now and double later, you are not showing a big hand. However, if you double now and bid your suit later, you are promising at least 17 HCP.

West	North	East	South
—	—	1♣	???

♠ AK632 ♡ Q652 ◇ K109 ♣ 6
Overcall 1♠, prepared to double at your next turn.

♠ J532 ♡ A9854 ◇ AKJ ♣ 9
Overcall 1♡, even with the indifferent suit.

♠ KJ74 ♡ AQJ73 ◇ AQ9 ♣ 2
You are strong enough to double now, and bid hearts later. Of course, if partner bids spades, you will be happy to raise.

TREAD LIGHTLY

Do not overcall at the two level in a mediocre five-card suit.

A two-level overcall is usually based on a six-bagger. When you have only a five-card suit, it should include at least three honors.

In fact, it is often better to pass than to venture to the two level with a shaky suit. The higher the level of the overcall, the more likely it is to end the auction. Too often, you will be the "lucky" recipient of a dummy whose trump "support" consists of a small singleton!

West	North	East	South
—	—	1♠	???

♠ 65　♡ K8642　♢ KQ5　♣ AJ10
Double. Overcalling 2♡ on this anemic suit is begging for trouble. Your minor-suit support is more than adequate for a flexible takeout double.

♠ J643　♡ A　♢ Q9652　♣ KQJ
Pass. These diamonds do not sparkle.

♠ 2　♡ 10875　♢ AKQ1086　♣ 73
Overcall 2♢ — these diamonds are brilliant.

SANDWICH OVERCALLS — YUMMY

When LHO opens 1♣ or 1◇, partner passes, and RHO responds in a new suit, your bid of either suit is not a cuebid — it is natural.

These are called "sandwich overcalls" because they are made in between two bidding opponents.

West	North	East	South
1♣	Pass	1♡	???

When LHO opened 1♣, he did not promise a good club suit. RHO's 1♡ response did not promise great hearts, either. Therefore, it is quite possible for you, the "fourth hand" to have length and strength in either of those suits. It would be a shame to have a great suit and not be able to show it — after all, bridge is a bidder's game. Here are two examples to clarify.

♠ A6 ♡ 63 ◇ J863 ♣ AKQJ9   Overcall 2♣

♠ 743 ♡ AQJ986 ◇ K97 ♣ 3   Overcall 2♡

By the way: Some players define these overcalls as cuebids, showing the two unbid suits. This is not necessary — with two-suited hands, you can double or bid the Unusual notrump.

THE MIGHTY JORDAN

After partner's opening bid is doubled, a jump to 2NT promises good trump support and at least 10 distribution points.

Responder does not need 2NT to show a strong balanced hand — with that, he redoubles. However, he does need a way to show a limit raise (or better), because after a double, a jump raise is weak. Jordan 2NT (alertable) fits the bill nicely.

Notice that responder is forcing the auction to the three level. He needs a nine-card fit to provide safety there. Therefore, he should have five cards in opener's minor, or four in the major.

West	North	East	South
Pass	1◇	Dbl	???

♠ 64 ♡ A8 ◇ K8762 ♣ K876   Bid 2NT

West	North	East	South
—	1♡	Dbl	???

♠ A95 ♡ KQ95 ◇ 10843 ♣ 72   Bid 2NT

MUCH ADO ABOUT NOTHING

You do not need a lot of points to make a "free bid."

When partner bids or doubles and RHO does not pass, you are "off the hook." Even if you choose to pass, partner will get another chance to bid.

Many players go one step further and take this to mean that you should only bid when you have "points." This is definitely not true. All you need is a reason to compete.

West	North	East	South
1♣	Dbl	1♠	???

♠ 64 ♡ K9542 ◇ 8762 ♣ 83　　　　　Bid 2♡

♠ 832 ♡ 75 ◇ AJ98　♣ 7542　　　　Bid 2◇

West	North	East	South
—	—	—	1◇
Pass	1NT	2♠	???

♠ 9 ♡ 875 ◇ AQ976 ♣ KQ105

Bid 3♣. Once partner denied a major, you must have a minor-suit fit. You do not want to defend 2♠.

A BID FOR ALL SEASONS

Stuck for a bid? Try a cuebid.

Too many players are intimidated by cuebids. You need not be. There are many good uses for the flexible cuebid in competitive auctions. It is often utilized when you don't have a stopper in the opponent's suit (if you had one, you would bid notrump yourself).

West	North	East	South
—	—	—	1♣
2♠	3♡	Pass	???

♠ 854 ♡ 105 ◇ AK4 ♣ AQ743
Cuebid 3♠. If partner has a spade stopper, you will be delighted to let him declare 3NT.

West	North	East	South
—	1◇	Pass	1♠
2♡	3◇	Pass	???

♠ AQ63 ♡ 742 ◇ A83 ♣ Q75
Cuebid 3♡. It would be silly to raise diamonds, which would bypass 3NT.

By the way: Any player can cuebid, but this type of cuebid is usually made by the side that opens.

BALANCING DIFFERENCES

In the balancing seat, some of your actions may be light. Others take on a completely different meaning.

Make sure you discuss this with your partner.

West	North	East	South
1 suit	Pass	Pass	???

May Be Light in the Balancing Seat

Double
Overcall at one level
Overcall at two level (nonjump)
Michaels cuebid

Completely Different Meaning

1NT now shows only 10-14 HCP.

2NT promises 19-21 HCP.
It is definitely not the Unusual notrump.

A jump overcall shows an opening bid with a six-card suit — it is NOT weak.

You open in a major, partner raises and RHO intervenes. A new suit below three of your major invites game.

This bid says nothing about your holding in the new suit. Therefore, it is both artificial and alertable.

This is not a "newfangled device," it is a necessary convention. When opener has a shapely minimum, he must be able to compete to three of his major without worrying about partner bidding on. Defining a bid of a new suit as a game try gives opener a way to show a better hand.

West	North	East	South
—	—	—	1♠
Pass	2♠	3♦	???

♠ AK8752 ♡ A8 ◇ Q95 ♣ Q6
Bid 3♡. Partner will jump to 4♠ with a maximum or bid 3♠ with a minimum.

♠ AQ964 ♡ 872 ◇ 6 ♣ AKJ9
3♡ again. Although you have great clubs, you can't bid 4♣ because that would commit you to game.

♠ AQJ754 ♡ KQ ◇ 54 ♣ J82
Bid 3♠. You are commanding partner to pass.

Chapter 11

I'LL HAVE A DOUBLE

THE VOB DOUBLE

With VOB, it is okay to double a 1♣ or 1◇ opening bid without a four-card major.

This is true even if you have three (rarely four) cards in opener's minor. Get your values off your chest now, while the auction is at the one level. The more imperfect your shape, the more HCP you need for your double.

West	North	East	South
—	—	1♣	???

♠ K97 ♡ A106 ◇ KQ74 ♣ J52
Double, even if you are vulnerable.

♠ AQ8 ♡ KJ4 ◇ A94 ♣ 7643
Double. Making a takeout double with four cards in RHO's suit does not thrill me either. Fair enough, but passing would accomplish nothing.

♠ K102 ♡ A95 ◇ AJ964 ♣ 53
Double. Your best chance for game is in a major suit

By the way: With a lot of strength in opener's minor, pass — unless of course you are strong enough for a 1NT overcall.

I'M NOT POSITIVE

Responder's double is negative only when partner opens one of a suit and RHO makes a natural overcall in a suit (even a jump).

On each auction, decide if the double is negative.

West	North	East	South
Pass	1♡	1NT	Dbl

No. East did not make a natural overcall in a **suit**.

West	North	East	South
—	1♣	2♣	Dbl

No. East's 2♣ was a cuebid, it was not **natural**.

West	North	East	South
1♢	1♠	2♣	Dbl

No. Your partner did not **open**.

West	North	East	South
—	1♢	1♠	Dbl

YES. South promises 6+ HCP and 4+ hearts.

I'LL DOUBLE THAT

If partner opens one of a suit and RHO makes an artificial two-suited overcall, responder's double promises 10+ HCP.

That's all it promises — you can have almost any distribution for this double. It should remind you of your redouble when partner opens and RHO doubles.

West	North	East	South
—	1♦	2♦	???

♠ J65 ♡ 7532 ◇ AKJ ♣ A87

Double. East's Michaels cuebid has left you in a quandary. You can't bid notrump without stoppers in the majors, and you have no suit to bid. All you can do for now is show your values. You hope that partner has the majors under control and can bid notrump.

West	North	East	South
—	1♡	2NT	???

♠ AK93 ♡ J7 ◇ J5 ♣ Q9762

Double. You are ready to double clubs. If partner can handle the diamonds, a bonanza is in store.

When you make a takeout double, and double the same suit again, the second double is still takeout.

Your first double showed a good hand, with shortness in the opponent's suit. Your second double does not change that fact, but it does show a much better hand. You are still eager to hear from partner.

The higher the level of the double, the more often partner will decide to pass. Nobody likes introducing a worthless four-card suit at the four or five level.

With the following hand, South should make a second takeout double on both auctions below:

♠ AQ74   ♡ 5   ◇ AQJ   ♣ KQ973

West	North	East	South
—	—	1♡	Dbl
Pass	2◇	2♡	???

West	North	East	South
—	—	2♡	Dbl
4♡	Pass	Pass	???

Strive to make lead-directing doubles
of the opponents' artificial bids.

A lead-directing double tells partner that you would
really like him to lead the suit that you doubled. There
are many times when it comes into play. Some are:

- RHO bids Stayman.

- RHO bids a Jacoby transfer.

- RHO responds 2◇ to a strong 2♣ opening.

- RHO bids *new minor* or *fourth-suit* forcing.

- RHO responds to Blackwood.

West	North	East	South
1NT	Pass	2♣	???

♠ J43   ♡ 7   ◇ 8652   ♣ AQJ85

Double. You must tell partner you want a club lead.

By the way: Lead-directing doubles do not apply
when the opponents:

- Bid Michaels; or,

- Make an artificial overcall of partner's 1NT.

E.L.C.D.

If RHO opens 1♡ or 1♠, and you have four cards in the unbid major, five diamonds and 12+ HCP, make a takeout double.

This approach is a lot more flexible than overcalling 2◇. It represents the only time that a double followed by a voluntary bid of a new suit does NOT show "the big double." Those "in the know" refer to these as **E**qual **L**evel **C**onversion **D**oubles (E.L.C.D.).

West	North	East	South
—	—	1♠	???

♠ A4 ♡ AK98 ◇ J10542 ♣ 85

Double, even though you have only two clubs. As long as partner does not bid 2♣, you are content. Even if he does, you don't have a problem. Simply convert his 2♣ bid to 2◇. You are still at the same (equal) two level, and you know you did not miss a heart fit. Perfect.

Because this agreement is not "standard," the 2◇ bid is alertable.

By the way: E.L.C.D. still apply after RHO opens with a major-suit preempt, but you need a better hand to double at a higher level.

She Needs to be Taken Out

After LHO opens, partner passes and RHO responds 1NT, your double is takeout of LHO's suit.

Even with a lot of HCP, you need good shape for this double. Both opponents have bid, which means that partner probably has practically nothing. Also, the fact that the opponents have not found a fit suggests that you may not have one either.

West	North	East	South
1♠	Pass	1NT	???

♠ K5 ♡ J875 ◇ KJ5 ♣ AQ62
Pass. 11 HCP, but your spade king is poorly placed, and your shape is boring — sit this one out.

♠ 7 ♡ A984 ◇ A1076 ♣ A863
Double — love that singleton and three quick tricks.

By the way: The above holds true whether or not the opponents are playing 1NT forcing.

No "Up the Line" This Time

If partner doubles 1♣ or 1♢, and you have both majors, do not respond up the line.

The concept of bidding up the line applies when partner **opens** 1♣ or 1♢. Because your one-level response is forcing, partner must bid again. Your goal is to make the most economical bid possible, so that your side has maximum room to find a fit.

However, when partner makes a takeout double, he does not have to bid again. For example, if you bid 1♡ in response to his double, he will only bid spades if he has at least five of them, and a very strong hand. So with both majors, respond 1♠. You can always bid hearts later without "reversing."

West	North	East	South
1♢	Dbl	Pass	1♠
2♢	Pass	Pass	???

♠ K1054 ♡ K1054 ♢ 763 ♣ 32

Bid 2♡. You do not want to sell out. Partner can pass or bid spades at the two level — how convenient.

Bidding 1♡ initially, and 2♠ now, would result in a 3♡ contract whenever partner prefers hearts.

ALIVE AND KICKING

When partner doubles for takeout and RHO redoubles, you don't need much of an excuse to bid — "points, schmoints."

Once three players have promised good hands, the fourth player — that's you — must be weak. However, that is no reason to bury your head in the sand. If you have something to say, speak right up.

West	North	East	South
1◇	Dbl	Rdbl	???

♠ J3 ♡ 5432 ◇ J5432 ♣ 84
Bid 1♡. Don't pass and risk hearing partner bid 1♠.

♠ KJ853 ♡ 85 ◇ 96 ♣ 9432
Bid 2♠. This preemptive jump shows a weak hand with a five-card suit. It will really disrupt the enemy and is safe because partner's double promised at least three spades.

♠ Q87 ♡ Q54 ◇ 8543 ♣ J65
Pass. If West also passes, partner must bid. You are ready to accept any suit that he chooses.

MAY THE FORCE BE WITH YOU

After partner's takeout double, the only forcing response is a cuebid.

Because a nonjump response in a suit shows 0-8 points, jump bids are needed to show invitational hands with 9-11 HCP. The cuebid is used to show at least 12 points.

West	North	East	South
1♣	Dbl	Pass	???

Cuebid 2♣ with all of these hands:

♠ 92 ♡ KQ98 ◇ K864 ♣ A107
If partner bids 2◇, you will bid 2♡.
If partner bids 2♡, you will jump to 4♡.
If partner bids 2♠, you will bid 2NT, inviting game.

♠ K972 ♡ K6 ◇ J764 ♣ AK3
If partner bids 2◇ or 2♡, you will bid 2♠, which is forcing. If he has four spades, you will play a spade game. If not, 3NT will be fine.

♠ J75 ♡ AK6 ◇ KQJ97 ♣ 54
Your hand is much too strong for an invitational 2◇ bid. If partner bids 2♡ or 2♠, you will force with 3◇.

Chapter 12

IMPRESSIVE
DECLARER PLAY

LOOK MA, NO TRUMPS

If notrump contracts frighten you — relax.

Many players cringe at the thought of declaring a notrump contract. They remember the devastating feeling of going down in 3NT when the opponents gleefully cashed the first five tricks.

As unpleasant as those memories may be, try not to overreact. In fact, **notrump contracts are easier to declare than suit contracts**.

A notrump contract is essentially a competitive race. Each side hopes to finish first by establishing its suit and cashing enough tricks to "win" the hand. In suit contracts, you have to think about trumps, short suits, long suits, ruffs, overruffs, etc.

When declaring a notrump contract:

- Count your guaranteed, immediate winners.
- Figure out how many more tricks you need.
- Select a suit that will provide those tricks.
- Decide how to cope with the suit led.

On your mark, get set, go.

Declarer should lead an honor for a finesse
only when he is eager to have it covered.

Contract: 3NT
Lead: ♠Q

North
♠ A
♡ J52
◇ 732
♣ 976432

West
♡ QJ104
♡ 8763
◇ J6
♣ QJ5

East
♠ K987
♡ Q9
◇ 109854
♣ K10

South
♠ 6532
♡ AK104
◇ AKQ
♣ A8

Declarer needed to finesse in hearts, so he led the
♡J at trick two. However, when East covered, South
was able to win only the ace, king and ten.

South should have led dummy's ♡2 and finessed his
♡10. The ♡Q would fall under the ace on the second
round, and he would win the ten, ace, king and **jack**.

GOOD GUYS, BAD GUYS

Declarer should be careful to prevent the "bad guy" from obtaining the lead.

On some hands, one defender has a suit to run. Here, declarer needs to protect his delicate spades.

Contract: 3NT
Lead: ♠7

North
♠ Q
♡ KQ5
◇ 7432
♣ A10943

South
♠ K86
♡ AJ4
◇ AJ85
♣ KJ2

When the ♠Q holds the trick, South knows that West has the ♠A. If declarer lets East in, a spade return will prove fatal. East is the dangerous opponent, so declarer executes an "avoidance play" against him.

South leads the ♣10 at trick two and lets it ride, willing to lose a trick to West — the safe opponent. Declarer now has nine sure tricks: one spade, three hearts, one diamond and at least four clubs.

When declaring a suit contract, counting losers is just the tip of the iceberg.

Contract: 4♠
Lead: ♡10

North
♠ 752
♡ A74
♢ AK3
♣ QJ32

South
♠ AKQJ86
♡ J6
♢ 874
♣ 84

Observe an expert in action: "Let's see. Spades are solid, but I could lose one heart, one diamond and the ace-king of clubs. I need to get rid of a diamond somewhere — clubs look like the only hope. That's the plan. Okay, I don't want a diamond shift, so I better go up with the ♡A.

"Might as well draw trumps. Oh — East only had one. Time out. I better lead a club right now, while dummy still has a trump. If I don't, I will never be able to get back to my hand to play clubs. As long as the honors are split, I'll have a club winner for my tenth trick."

How Do I Ruff Thee?

Don't send a boy to do a man's job.

Contract: 4♡
Lead: ♣7

North
♠ 65
♡ A10
◇ Q97654
♣ Q42

South
♠ AK92
♡ QJ9876
◇ 83
♣ A

After winning the ♣A, you intend to ruff two spades in dummy. You are willing to concede the ♡K, along with the two inevitable diamond losers. Cash the ♠AK and lead a small spade You ruff it with dummy's ♡10, but East overruffs with the ♡K and returns a trump. Down one!

There is a foolproof way to assure the contract. You must ruff the small spade with dummy's ♡A! You can then return to your hand by ruffing a club. Now, ruff your last spade with that lovely ♡10, not caring if you are overruffed. Making four.

The fact that your trump suit is weak should not prevent you from drawing them.

Contract: 4♠
Lead: ♡J

North
♠ 8532
♡ 4
♢ AKJ10
♣ K642

South
♠ 9764
♡ AKQ
♢ Q865
♣ AJ

West	*North*	*East*	*South*
—	—	—	1NT
Pass	2♣	Pass	2♠
Pass	4♠	All pass	

Wouldn't you just hate to have a winner ruffed? Win the heart lead and lead a trump immediately. As long as they divide 3-2, you are cold (if they divide 4-1, even Houdini could not make the hand).

Even with a long, strong trump suit —
don't always rush to draw trumps.

North

Contract: 4♠
Lead: ♡10

♠ KJ743
♡ Q72
◇ 53
♣ 763

West

♠ —
♡ 109863
◇ A9862
♣ Q84

East

♠ A2
♡ AK54
◇ 1074
♣ J1092

South

♠ Q109865
♡ J
◇ KQJ
♣ AK5

East won the opening lead with his ♡K. He shifted to
the ♣J, West encouraging with the eight. South was
not blinded by his 11 trumps. He won the ♣A and led
the ◇K. West won his ◇A and returned a club, but
declarer was in control. He won his ♣K, cashed the
◇Q and discarded dummy's last club on the ◇J. If
declarer had drawn trumps first, the defense would
have set up a club trick while they still had the ◇A.

Last is best.

When you have a dubious holding in a suit, you should try to force the opponents to lead that suit. That insures that your side will play last.

	North	
Contract: 4♡	♠ A9	
Lead: ♠K	♡ KJ754	
	◇ J543	
	♣ K3	

West		East
♠ KQ63		♠ J10754
♡ 86		♡ 2
◇ A109		◇ Q72
♣ 10654		♣ QJ97

	South
	♠ 82
	♡ AQ1093
	◇ K86
	♣ A82

Declarer won the ♠A, drew trumps and eliminated his side's clubs by cashing the ace and king and ruffing the third round. He then exited with dummy's ♠9. Now the opponents were endplayed — forced to give declarer a ruff-sluff or lead diamonds. Voilà.

A Wolf in Sheep's Clothing

When the opening leader is about to win the first trick, declarer should "signal" with a high card if he wants the suit continued.

The best way to induce your LHO to do what *you* want is to signal your attitude as if you were his partner. This deceptive play is called a falsecard.

                    North
                    ♡ 54<u>3</u>
        West   *East*
        ♡ <u>A</u>KJ6   ♡ 108<u>7</u>
                    South
                    ♡ Q92

West leads the ♡A. If South plays the ♡2, West knows that East's seven is his lowest card, and that he does not want the suit continued.

That is not the message declarer wants West to receive. Declarer is dying for West to continue hearts, and set up his ♡Q. Therefore, South should "signal" by playing his ♡9 — just as he would if he were West's partner and liked hearts. Now, West is likely to believe that East started with ♡Q72 and will play right into South's hand. Ha, we fooled him.

When playing a slam, count winners rather than losers.

Contract: 6♡!!
Lead: ♠10

North
♠ A7653
♡ 5
♢ QJ9543
♣ 10

West
♠ K1098
♡ 3
♢ K7
♣ KJ8543

East
♠ J42
♡ 9742
♢ 10862
♣ Q9

South
♠ Q
♡ AKQJ1086
♢ A
♣ A762

After some serious overbidding, you arrive in 6♡.

Stop and count your winners before you play: seven heart tricks, three side aces and a club ruff in dummy. That's eleven. Your only hope for a 12th trick is that West led away from the ♠K, so that your ♠Q becomes a winner. Lo and behold, it does! Guess it wasn't such a bad slam after all.

Finesses lose half the time. Don't take
every one that you see.

Contract: 6♠
Lead: ◇3

North
♠ Q109
♡ 8
◇ AQ4
♣ QJ9876

South
♠ AKJ8764
♡ A742
◇ 62
♣ —

You have seven spade winners in your hand plus the
two red aces. By ruffing three hearts in dummy, you
have 12 easy tricks.

You've done well to bid a slam with only 23 HCP —
don't be greedy. If you finesse the ◇Q and East wins
the king, a trump shift will limit you to eleven tricks.
That would be ridiculous. Grab the ◇A, cross-ruff
hearts and clubs and score up your slam.

THIS DUCK IS NO FOWL

Lose your losers early.

When declarer has an inevitable loser in a suit, he should invariably lose it sooner rather than later. This variation of the holdup play is referred to as a "duck," and its purpose is to preserve entries.

Contract: 6♠
Lead: ◇J

North
♠ 64
♡ A94
◇ Q3
♣ A97643

South
♠ AKQJ932
♡ K72
◇ A
♣ 85

You have 11 sure winners, and as long as clubs divide 3-2, you can develop a twelfth. Win the diamond lead, draw trumps and lose (duck) a club. You can win any return in your hand and lead a club to dummy's ace. Now, ruff out the opponent's one remaining club, establishing that suit. Cross to dummy's ♡A, discard your heart loser on a club winner, and claim.

Chapter 13

THE DEFENSE
NEVER RESTS

A Very Overrated Lead

Don't lead a doubleton unless you have
a good reason.

Why? Your short suit is often an opponent's long suit.
Don't start out by helping declarer develop it.

Yes, a singleton is also a short suit, but it has one
great advantage. Once you lead it — all gone.

In general, leading a doubleton does not work out
well. The absolute worst times to lead one are:

- Except in partner's suit, when your doubleton
  contains exactly one honor: Kx, Qx, Jx, 10x.
- When you do not need or want a ruff; e.g.,
  your trump holding is J109x, QJ10.

Obviously, you are always eager to lead a doubleton
in partner's long suit (five or more). Here are some
other good reasons to lead a doubleton.

- You have a sequence: AK, KQ, QJ, J10, 109.
- The auction screamed for a lead of this suit
  (the opponents bid all the other ones).
- You have trump control (Axx, Ax or Kxx). If
  declarer can't draw your trumps immediately,
  your chances of obtaining a ruff are good.

PARTNER, WHEREFORE ART THOU?

When your only hope is to "find partner," reject the suit(s) he has "denied."

North

Contract: 3NT
Lead: ♣5

North
♠ A92
♡ AQ
♢ KQJ1065
♣ 108

West
♠ Q75
♡ 9752
♢ 843
♣ Q75

East
♠ 1064
♡ J10
♢ A97
♣ KJ643

South
♠ KJ83
♡ K8643
♢ 2
♣ A92

North	South
1♢	1♡
3♢	3NT

It would have been futile for West to lead spades, the unbid major. If East had long spades, he would have overcalled 1♠. However, an overcall in clubs would have required going to the two level — not so easy.

West led a club, and once the ♣A was knocked out, the defense was in control. East was able to run the suit when he got in with the ♢A. Down one!

SLAM KILLING

Lead passively against a grand slam or 6NT.
Lead aggressively against all other slams.

Your goal against grand slams:

> Make the safest lead possible, which is often
> a trump. Exception: if you think the opponents
> might be missing an ace, or that partner has
> a void, you should try to "find" him.

Your goal against 6NT:

> Again, avoid giving anything away. If the
> opponents have shown balanced hands,
> a top-of-nothing lead is fine. Obviously, a
> three-card sequence is a great first choice.

> However, if either opponent has shown a long
> suit, you must adopt an attacking mentality.

Your goal against six of a suit:

> Set up trick(s) for your side before declarer can
> discard his losers. Lead aggressively — this is
> the time to lay down an ace or lead away from
> a king or queen. You should usually avoid the
> passive trump lead.

THE HCP DETECTIVE

As soon as dummy is tabled, each defender should add dummy's HCP to his own.

By keeping the auction in mind, you will be well placed to zero in on the remaining HCP.

This is easiest to apply when declarer opens 1NT, or the auction pinpoints his high-card range.

Contract: 3NT
Lead: ◇J

North
♠ 63
♡ A9
◇ Q62
♣ KJ10954

East (You)
♠ 1098742
♡ KJ108
◇ A
♣ A6

South	*North*
1NT	3NT

To begin, add your 12 HCP to the 10 HCP in dummy. Add this 22 to declarer's 15-17. Partner is left with 1-3 HCP. He led the ◇J, so he can't have more than a queen. Your only hope is that it is the ♡Q, and that you can set up three heart tricks before your ♣A is knocked out. Win your ◇A, return the ♡J, and pray.

When declarer attacks a suit and you have two stoppers, it is often correct to duck.

Contract: 3NT
Lead: ♠J

North
♠ K65
♡ 63
◇ 743
♣ K10985

West
♠ J10974
♡ 872
◇ Q108
♣ 72

East
♠ 8
♡ QJ109
◇ J962
♣ AQ43

South
♠ AQ32
♡ AK54
◇ AK5
♣ J6

South won the ♠Q and led the ♣J. If East wins, declarer is in control. He can win the (obvious) heart return and lead his ♣6 to knock out East's ♣A. South has three club tricks and will emerge with an overtrick.

East must duck the ♣J and win the second club. Declarer no longer has a club to lead, and dummy's clubs are dead. South will take only three spades, two hearts, two diamonds and one club — down one.

THE WAITING GAME

When you have the opportunity to overruff with a sure trump trick — don't.

Spades are trump.

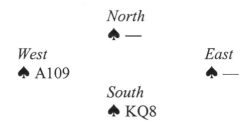

> *North*
> ♠ 54
> ♡ 86
>
> *West*   *East*
> ♠ A109   ♠ 62
> ♡ —   ♡ 109
> ◇ 7
>
> *South*
> ♠ KQJ8
> ♡ —

East leads the ♡10. When South ruffs with the ♠J, West must NOT overruff — he should discard the ◇7. The relevant trumps will be:

> *North*
> ♠ —
>
> *West*   *East*
> ♠ A109   ♠ —
>
> *South*
> ♠ KQ8

West is now assured of two trump tricks.

When there is no hope remaining in the side suits, try to promote a trump trick.

Contract: 4♡
Lead: ♠Q

North
♠ 643
♡ K542
◇ AKQ7
♣ AK

West
♠ QJ9
♡ J
◇ 10842
♣ J8542

East
♠ AK107
♡ 1098
◇ 963
♣ 1076

South
♠ 852
♡ AQ763
◇ J5
♣ Q93

The defense took the first three spade tricks. At trick four, East had to decide what to lead. Looking at dummy, he saw no hope in either clubs or diamonds. Accordingly, East led a fourth spade, hoping West could ruff in with a trump honor. Lo and behold, declarer had to overruff West's ♡J with dummy's ♡K, promoting East's 10-9-8 of trumps for the setting trick.

Wait to cover the LAST of touching honors that are led from dummy.

North
♠ QJ94

West
♠ 1063

East (You)
♠ K75

South
♠ A82

Declarer begins setting up this suit by leading the queen from the board. If you (East) play the king now, South will win his ace and continue by leading the two to finesse dummy's nine. Your side will never take a trick in this suit.

Notice the difference when you duck the queen. It holds, and South leads the jack from the board. Now, you play the king and declarer wins his ace. Partner's ten is high — nicely done.

By the way: If after winning the queen, declarer continues by leading the four from dummy, you will obviously play low. As long as you wait to "cover the last honor," South must lose a spade trick.

GLOSSARY

1NT Response to Major — Refers to the standard treatment (6-10 HCP) as well as 1NT forcing.

2/1 Auctions — References in this book apply to both the traditional 10+ HCP and the two-over-one game-forcing style.

2♣ Opening — A strong, artificial and forcing opening bid used with powerhouse hands when playing weak two-bids. Opener either has a long suit, or a balanced hand too strong to open 2NT.

4-3-3-3 — That distribution, the four-card suit is unspecified.

5-5 — At least five cards in each of two suits.

Alertable — In duplicate bridge, some artificial calls made by a player must be "alerted" by his partner to inform the opponents that the action was not natural.

Artificial Bid — A bid that does not promise the suit that was named.

Balanced Distribution — A hand with no singleton or void, and at most one doubleton. Balanced patterns are: 4-3-3-2, 4-3-3-3 and 5-3-3-2.

Balancing Seat — A player is said to be in the balancing seat when his pass would end the auction. One should often try to reopen rather than allow the opponents to play in a low-level contract.

Bid — 1♣ through 7NT. Does not include pass, double or redouble.

"The Board" — Refers to dummy.

Call — Any bid, pass, double or redouble.

Cold — Slang for a contract that is sure to make.

"Colors" — Vulnerability. In duplicate, red stands for vulnerable, black for nonvulnerable.

Control (noun) — A holding that prevents the opponents from winning the first two tricks in a suit.

Count, as in "18 count" — 18 HCP.

Cuebid — An artificial, forcing bid in the opponent's suit. Also, a bid of a new suit after the trump suit has been established (as a slam try).

Dbl — Double.

Distribution — The number of cards in each suit.

Distribution Points — The total of a player's HCP and his "short-suit" points after a fit is found.

Draw(ing) Trumps — Leading trumps, to remove as many as possible from the opponents' hands.

Duck — To play a small card, surrendering a trick you might have won.

Entry — A holding that provides access to a hand. Efficient use of entries is crucial for both sides.

Favorable Vulnerability — You are not vulnerable, the opponents are.

Fit — A term refferring to the partnership's combined assets with respect to a suit, usually trump.

HCP — High-card points.

Intermediates — Middle cards such as the 10, 9, 8.

Jacoby 2NT — Artificial, forcing raise of opener's major. Opener shows a singleton if he has one.

Jacoby Transfer — Used in response to notrump opening bids, or a natural notrump overcall. A diamond bid promises heart length, while a heart response shows at least five spades. Opener must bid the suit responder has "shown."

Law of Total Tricks ("The Law") — You are always safe bidding to the level equal to your side's number of trumps. Very helpful when judging whether to bid on in competitive auctions. Based on the concept that "Trump Length is Everything."

LHO — Left-hand opponent.

Limit Raise — Responder's invitational raise from one to three of a suit, promising 11-12 distribution points and trump support.

Michaels Cuebid — An overcall in the opponent's suit that shows at least five cards in two suits. The emphasis is on the unbid major(s).

Natural — A bid which promises the suit named.

New Minor Forcing — After opener's rebid of 1NT or 2NT, responder's bid in an unbid minor asks opener about his major-suit length. Responder usually has a five-card major with at least game-invitational values.

Open — Make the first bid.

Preempt — A jump bid based on a long suit and weak hand. The intention is to deprive the opponents of bidding space, making it harder for them to reach their optimal contract.

Quick Trick — A high-card holding that will usually result in a trick (also known as defensive tricks).
   AK = 2; AQ = 1 ½; A = 1; KQ = 1; Kx = ½.

Reverse — Opener's rebid at the two level in a suit that is higher-ranking than his first bid. It shows at least 17 points and promises five or six cards in his first suit. This topic causes more anxiety than any other one.

RHO — Right-hand opponent.

The Rule of 20 — Used to evaluate whether to open borderline hands in first and second seat. Add the length of your two longest suits to your HCP. With 20 or more, open the bidding in a suit at the one level.

Shape — See "Distribution."

Side Suit(s) — Any suit other than trumps.

Signoff — A bid intended to end the auction. Sometimes referred to as a *drop-dead bid*.

Splinter Bid — Conventional jump into a short suit (0 or 1 card), promising good support for partner and values for game or slam.

Stopper — A card or combination of cards that prevents the opponents from running a suit in a notrump contract.

Tenace — A combination of non-consecutive honors. Some examples are KJ and AQ.

Thrump Double — Made in the hope that partner has a stopper as well as a suitable hand to bid 3NT.

Transfer — In this book, a Jacoby transfer.

Unfavorable Vulnerability — You are vulnerable, the opponents are not.

Unusual Notrump Overcall — A method of showing length in the two lower unbid suits after an opponent opens the bidding.

VOB — Stands for: Enough **V**alues to **O**pen the **B**idding, but not much more.

xx — Small cards; in this case, exactly two.

Yarborough — A hand with no card above a nine.

RECOMMENDED READING

If you enjoyed *Marty Sez,* you might want to consider ordering the following books. (Ordering details can be found on the next page.) Bridge books make a great gift for your card-playing friends and family.

**Free shipping if your order includes
any of Marty's hardcover books.**

BY MARTY BERGEN

If I Knew Then, What I Know Now
   (not bridge)   Hardcover — $15.95

Marty Sez   Hardcover — $17.95

Points Schmoints!   Hardcover — $19.95
   (1996 Book of the Year)

More Points Schmoints!   Hardcover — $19.95

* Special: Buy both *Points Schmoints* books $35 *

Negative Doubles $9.95

Introduction to Negative Doubles $6.95

**Upon request, all books by Marty
will be sent with personalized autograph.**

ALSO BY MARTY BERGEN

Better Bidding — Uncontested Auctions $11.95

Better Bidding — Competitive Bidding $11.95

Marty's reference book on conventions ~~$9.95~~ $6.50

BY LARRY COHEN

Play Bridge with Larry Cohen—1999 Life Master Pairs
Day 1, 2 and 3 **CD ROM** ~~$29.95~~ $26 each
"Over My Shoulder" style with many deals.

♠ ♡ ♢ ♣

To order by credit card (all cards welcome) call:
1-800-386-7432

Or send a check or money order (U.S. dollars) to:
**Marty Bergen
9 River Chase Terrace
Palm Beach Gardens, FL 33418-6817**

Or E-mail Marty directly at
mbergen@adelphia.net

Please include $3 postage and handling, but:
Postage is free **if your order includes
any of Marty's hardcover books.**